FIFTY YEARS IN ST JOHN AMBULANCE

Ray Pennock

Published by Lulu,
Morrisville NC, USA and Putney, London, UK

Typeset in 12pt Georgia

ISBN - 978-1-4457-8325-3

PUBLISHER'S DISCLAIMER
The author accepts all liability for any actions arising in connection with events and/or individuals mentioned in this book and in respect of the photographs herein.

ACKNOWLEDGEMENT

I would like to thank my fellow St John Ambulance Officer, Robert Chantler for all his help and encouragement in making my dream of a book a reality.

1

THE EARLY YEARS   (1957 to 1972)

At the age of 15, still at school and with rock and roll as the new love of my life, the only place to be was the coffee bar at the Duke's Head crossroads in Addlestone High Street. I still can remember riding through the High Street (on a push bike) singing "Heartbreak Hotel" at the top of my voice.

Youth was starting to get bad press; we got blamed for everything (sounds familiar) and I felt like it would be good to show them that we were not all teddy boys, so I looked around to do something good that I could enjoy.

A couple of my school chums were in the Scouts, another one was in the Boy's Brigade, and someone else was a Cadet in St John Ambulance. Well as both the Scouts and the Boy's Brigade uniform consisted of short trousers, but St John had just changed to long trousers no contest. One had to think of one's image; a rock & roller in shorts. No chance, especially with my knees, and that's why I joined St John.

Addlestone Cadet Division, boys only (the girls met on another night) met at the old lodge which was part of St.Paul's School and was run by a very able man, Mr Tim Elerby. He taught us all the first aid we needed to know, with lots of stretcher work, and if you tied a granny knot well...... But more, he tolerated our high jinks, like one night I was tied to a stretcher then turned upside down and carried down two flights of stairs; my only injury being my grazed nose rubbing on some of the treads. He also tolerated the length and styles of our hair, and he had our loyalty.

 My mum was quite pleased about me joining, though did not really understand what it was all about. My dad just grunted and said "Just remember son, don't volunteer for anything." Little did he know, or me for that matter. As for the uniform, the grey shirt with chrome buttons, a tie, which we were banned from tying into a Windsor knot (that was a teddy boy thing), a white lanyard and a black beret with a pom-pom on the top, and of course the long grey trousers -- real cool!

Addlestone Division was one of many in the area. Chertsey, Egham, Woodham & Byfleet, Airscrew, Walton & Weybridge, Hersham, Esher, Sunbury, Cobham and Staines were just a few. Only two had an ambulance and Addlestone was not one of them. So duties tended to be very local, and in Addlestone the highlight of the year was the annual week-long fun fair held in a large field at Crockford Bridge Farm, now the Wyevale Garden Centre, next to the Black Horse pub. We would have to erect a large tent as a first aid station -- it usually rained whilst we did this -- and the duty was always busy with injuries from both the fair and the pub. Most of the other events were fetes and of course the Remembrance Day parade, and who could forget the day the St John flag got stuck in the top of the entrance of the altar and was left hanging there all through the ceremony.

I left school at sixteen, and started working at a garage (Moore's of Weybridge; a Ford main dealer) in the parts department, and this was my occupation until I was made redundant in 1985 as a parts manager of a Fiat main dealer.

Reaching the age of seventeen, I moved up to the Adults with one other, Mick Ryan. The Division met at the church hall next to Bundy's garage (now long gone) and we received our new uniform, a heavy woollen black jacket and trousers with a thin white stripe down the leg, a thick black leather belt, water bottle and a white haversack. These last two items were always checked at annual inspection, and of course a peaked hat.

Now we started to look the part, and to our joy a year later we were given an ambulance, a new one, a gift from a local charity, It was a Bedford, a bit like an old army lorry with a crocodile bonnet, painted black with the rear doors white and a chrome bell on the front. This opened up the range of duties we could attend; the main one being motor bike scrambles at Pirbright. Oh, the smell of Castrol R, the oil the bikes used, the dust on the hot summer's day, the mud in the winter, the cold and the occasional snow on the annual Boxing day meeting (it got rid of the hangover though).

We also covered horse shows and air displays at Fairoaks aerodrome; in fact my first serious incident occurred in 1962 at one of these air shows. A huge crowd had turned up as it was the first ever female wing-walker display, with a young lady on the wing of a Tiger Moth aeroplane. All the flyers were instructed not to fly over the crowds, but no-one had thought to tell the people doing the model aeroplane flying display. These models were quite large, some with over a six foot wingspan. Anyhow, one guy lost control of his plane and it crashed into the crowd. We saw it happen and I was first on scene.

On arriving, I found a woman lying on the floor with a lot of blood all over the grass. She had been struck in the leg by the nylon propeller of the aeroplane. Sliding my hand under her calf, I felt something warm and sticky (the days before gloves) and on lifting her leg up I was shocked to see she had a twelve inch gash in the calf muscle and I could see right inside to the bones; the whole wound was covered in model aircraft fuel and must have hurt like hell, but she just lay there telling her husband and young daughter to go and collect other children from the riding stables and to stop panicking. As soon as we had loaded her into the ambulance and shut the doors, only then did she start to scream with the pain.

I was amazed how she had controlled the pain in front of her husband and daughter

Another regular duty was at the Runnymede Pleasure Park by the Thames near Egham. This was done on a rota between the local Divisions and on a hot summer's day we would be very busy dealing with thirty to forty casualties -- everything from fish hooks in fingers, standing on broken glass in the river, wasp and bee stings and occasionally, Primus stoves blowing up. Once we had a body in the river but as it appeared to have been in there for some time, we resisted doing any first aid on him, though we had to treat the poor fisherman who, while sitting fishing, had the body slowly float up from the depths in front of him. Interestingly if you pulled out a body on the Surrey side you could claim 1/ 9p (old money), if it was on the Middlesex side it was 2/ 6 pence, but at least we could spend up to 1/9p food allowance each at the café that was there. That was our payment for the duty 1/9p each. The first aid hut was unbelievable. For a start it was very small, and one spent the first hour removing the spiders and their webs. If you had more then two casualties you were in trouble, and if it rained, it leaked and also you were the only people there in the whole park.

Addlestone Division had about seven members and was run by Mr Pim King, his wife Audrey running the Nursing Division. One member who had quite an influence on me was Frank Saige. He had been a member for some time and he taught me so much; not only first aid but about life. He was married with three young sons, had worked on a farm were he had been poisoned with a pesticide and he was in fact slowly dying from kidney failure. He lived every day to its full and taught me to be glad to be alive. Later on he had a transplant which gave him an extra ten years of life, and when he was finally dying, he said to me "I can go now; my boys are sixteen, eighteen and twenty. If I had died ten years ago they'd have only been six, eight and ten -- they can look after themselves and their mum" -- what a great guy!

Another new member was Howard Quinnell, and he, Mick Ryan, Frank and I made up the competition team that entered the annual competition held at Airscrew and Petters. One evening when training, our team was given a scenario of an unconscious casualty in a darkened room filled with gas, and to make it realistic, someone turned on the gas tap. As we entered, the three of us could smell the gas. Unfortunately the last one could not so he struck a match to give us some light. The first one out of the room was the casualty followed by us three leaving poor Frank still holding the match. But one of the best memories I have of Frank is when in a competition he was attacked by an actor carrying a meat hook. You were supposed to talk to the man to get him to lay down the meat hook, Frank being Frank hit him! That stopped the test and when asked why he had done it just said "If anyone attacked me like that, that's how I would react". He was the one that taught me, "Remember in this organisation we all get the same pay no matter what you have on your shoulders."

As we were one of the Voluntary Aid organisations, Frank and I were invited to attend a lecture on our role in case of a nuclear attack given by the Civil Defence and we were told what we should do in the run up to a forthcoming attack. They showed a film with people putting up newspapers in their windows and filling up their baths with water and stocking up with food; all this with a three minute warning. The final straw for us two was when they showed how we would be notified, sirens, rockets or maroons would be used or some other means. They then showed us a film clip of a Civil Defence warden on a push-bike blowing a whistle, who must have been at least seventy years old. That was it. I turned to Frank and said "That's why they want us here, to treat him when he has a heart attack". We were then asked to leave as we were not taking the evening seriously.

****

In January 1964, Sir Winston Churchill died and a request to the Home Counties from London District was received for help at the state funeral. My first major ceremonial London duty -- we left Addlestone at three thirty a.m., arriving at our station by four thirty at East Cheep in the City of London. It was pitch black; hardly any street lights, and you could just make out small groups of St John by the glowing of cigarettes. As for the cold wind that came off the Thames, I have never felt so cold; thank God we had our trench coats to wear. Frank and I had our coats hung over our shoulders, and at six thirty, a London District officer finally appeared and walking up to us two said "You two, what, do you think you are in the Austrian army wearing your coats like that?" "If we were," said Frank, "at least the officers would be on time, not two hours late."

That was the start of the duty, and when they asked for a stretcher party. Frank said "That's for us" and us four from Addlestone found ourselves with a stretcher, out of the wind in a shop entrance. He certainly knew the ropes. Just as the cortège was passing a soldier collapsed and we missed seeing anything as we were busy loading our man onto the stretcher. How many times has that happened since! We arrived back home at four pm just in time to watch it on our small black and white TV, and guess who promptly fell asleep?

****

In January 1964, Sir Winston Churchill died and a request to the Home Counties from London District was received for help at the state funeral. My first major ceremonial London duty -- we left Addlestone at three thirty a.m., arriving at our station by four thirty at East Cheep in the City of London. It was pitch black; hardly any street lights, and you could just make out small groups of St John by the glowing of cigarettes. As for the cold wind that came off the Thames, I have never felt so cold; thank God we had our trench coats to wear. Frank and I had our coats hung over our shoulders, and at six thirty, a London District officer finally appeared and walking up to us two said "You two, what, do you think you are in the Austrian army wearing your coats like that?" "If we were," said Frank, "at least the officers would be on time, not two hours late."

That was the start of the duty, and when they asked for a stretcher party. Frank said "That's for us" and us four from Addlestone found ourselves with a stretcher, out of the wind in a shop entrance. He certainly knew the ropes. Just as the cortège was passing a soldier collapsed and we missed seeing anything as we were busy loading our man onto the stretcher. How many times has that happened since! We arrived back home at four pm just in time to watch it on our small black and white TV, and guess who promptly fell asleep?

The next major event I attended was the opening of the J.F. Kennedy Memorial at Runnymede by the Queen. Unfortunately I had been drinking the night before, and being slightly dehydrated, together with standing to attention for quite a long time, and with the hot sun on my neck and wearing the full black uniform suddenly I felt a bit odd. Everything seemed in a dream, voices sounded like they were in cotton wool, then my eye sight developed tunnel vision. The next I knew was I was being carried off on a stretcher -- Ooops! Another event missed -- still learnt a lesson; don't drink too much the night before a large duty.

A County officer who will always stick in my mind was County Sergeant Major Nick Carter. What a character; ex-RSM and an imposing sight at over six foot, his uniform immaculate, the peak of his hat over his eyes and his silver capped stick he always carried on the parade ground. You would be standing to attention when suddenly a voice behind you would say "Am I hurting you?" "No Sergeant Major." "Well you ought to because I am standing on your hair!" But his best remarks were reserved for the officers when they fell in on the parade ground; try keeping a straight face when you could hear him saying behind you "What a bloody shower, can't march to save their lives, God help us" etc.

One day at a big parade, he was talking to some of us and told us that he had written to NHQ *[National HQ, London]* about removing the order that women had to curtsey when he saluted them. NHQ had written back with a very curt, "mind your own business." He said to us not to laugh at anything that happens today, but just watch. The inspecting officer (a rather mature lady) walked up to him. Nick came to attention and saluted as only he knew how. She just nodded. He stopped her, and in a loud voice pointed out she should curtsey. Poor lady -- she had to be helped up from the position. Funnily enough that regulation was changed within nine months.

In the spring of 1965 I dealt with my first major incident whilst not on duty; an RTA. While driving my girlfriend Kate home to Ewell one evening (she was not in St John), we were travelling along the Hersham dual carriageway when a motorcyclist overtook us at speed. I made the remark "He's in a hurry to kill himself." At the end of the road, it narrowed to a little hump back bridge and as we arrived, we saw an Austin A30 with a motor bike buried into its front. Coming over the bridge, my head lights picked up the rider lying in the gutter about fifteen yards further on. OH HELP! Pulling up, and as I got my first aid box out of the boot of the car, I told Kate to go and check the occupants of the car and let me know how they were, and walked up to this lifeless body lying in the road.

I felt panic, numbness, and wanted to be any where rather then here, but then the training kicked in. "Hello, are you OK?" I heard myself ask. He groaned. Great, he must be breathing. In those days we were taught the three B's (breathing, bleeding and breaks), and as I knelt down beside him I saw a river of blood starting to flow down the gutter. What a mess! His helmet had come off leaving a 1 inch wide gash right across his forehead. He was bleeding from his eyes, nose, mouth and one ear, his right arm was in a very odd position and as I checked I saw that his right femur was sticking out of his clothing. Just then a woman from a nearby house ran up saying that she had called the ambulance and the police. Great! At least that had been taken care of. Now I had to try to stop the bleeding but this woman started yelling at me. "Don't touch him, leave him alone!"

I tried to explain I was in St John but she just kept yelling at me. Finally I turned round to her and told her to f*** off. She went away complaining about the youth of today and their swearing. By this time, Kate came back to say that the couple in the car were not injured, so I asked her if she would stay with them as the ambulance was on its way. Back to the casualty, he now wanted to get up and walk home. Just then the police turned up, and in my naivety I thought they would take over the treatment. WRONG! All I got was "Do you know what you are doing son?" "Yes I'm a St John member." "That's all right then. Here's our first aid kit, looks like you need it. We will go and sort out the traffic."

Finally the ambulance arrived and I assisted with the loading of the casualty. Now to clear up and collect my first aid box, I could not find it. What thieving rat bag has nicked it? The police returned and I explained about my kit. They had it in their car. I found Kate, and decided to get her home. On arriving home, her father was waiting up as she should have been home over one and a half hours earlier and doubted my story until I rolled down my sleeve to find it was covered in blood. Unfortunately I learned later that the motorcyclist died on the way to hospital.

They always say that you remember the first major incident you treat, and in my case it's true. Things I learnt that night -- don't tempt fate by making comment, bystanders do not act the same as when in a first aid competition, don't expect the police to help you with first aid, your training does kick in when faced with a serious incident, and if it is their day to die they will die; all the first aider can do is their best.

In 1967, I married Kate and we bought a house in Knaphill, which was eight miles away from the Division but I still turned up regularly for training and duties, and in April the following year our daughter, Samantha (Sam) was born. Also, Mick Ryan got married and moved to Windlesham, but we both carried on as members of Addlestone, though not turning up every week.

****

1970 saw our son Neil born and with two young children St John was put on the back burner. Recently I found my old duty book in which I kept a record of what I had done. In 1970 I attended eight events, and seven in 1971, one of which I have painful memories to this day.

It was the only time there was a motorbike scramble held at Longcross and it took place on the heath land by Chobham Clump (so named because of the clump of tall pine trees on a hill, now sadly gone) and the ground was mainly sand and covered by heather and gorse bushes. It was a lovely hot summers day and everything was going quite well until four of us were carrying an injured rider on a stretcher back to the start/finish line where the ambulances were stationed. One thing I did not know was that heather tends to grow to the same height, however uneven the ground, and as we approached the ambulance, I suddenly stepped onto fresh air and disappeared down into a three foot deep trench. On landing, I heard a loud crack and felt a sharp pain in my left ankle. Emerging from the hole to a cheer from the nearby crowd, it proved that you can guarantee that if you make fool of yourself it will be in front of the public. Thank goodness the others had managed to save the rider and not drop him on top of me. You know how it is when you are embarrassed you carry on as if it's an everyday occurrence, so I picked up my side of the stretcher and loaded him into the ambulance. Now taking time to examine myself, I found my ankle was swollen up and very painful and being a good first aider I spent the rest of the day treating myself -- RICE. *[Treatment for sprains: Rest, Ice, Comfortable Support, Elevate]*

Previously at work, one of my workmates had fallen off a ladder at home and injured his ankle. He had gone to hospital, been operated on and they had messed up, and now he was going to be with a walking stick for the rest of his life. Also you know how bad we are at looking after ourselves, well, I was certain that all I had was a badly sprained ankle. If it had been a casualty, I would have sent them in for an X-ray. Now at the age of sixty plus I have a collapsed ankle, and a fallen arch and I can tell anyone when it's going to rain as it aches beforehand, and of course I also have a limp.

Prior to June 1972 I had only attended four duties that year, but one of those four was the turning point of my time in Addlestone. Previously, in 1971 both Pim and Audrey King had resigned from St John after falling out with CHQ, *[County HQ, Guildford]* about what we did not know, and then things started to go downhill. We (Mick and I) would turn up to find that the meeting had been cancelled but they had not told us, or if there were more then five of us then we would do some training otherwise it was just sitting around talking.

****

A request from Airscrew Division for first aiders saw me in 1971 attending the rehearsal and the Trooping of the Colour in London, and I was very impressed with the mobile first aid unit they had. But the duty that was to change my life was in February 1972.

Airscrew Division had asked us for first aiders to go with them to a demonstration in London, the coming Saturday. My First Demo! And what a demo! The shooting of thirteen people the month before by the army in Northern Ireland during a riot was now being called "Bloody Sunday". We arrived mid-afternoon and were stationed at the end of Downing Street on King Charles Square. The unit was set up and we now just waited to see what was going to happen. I had never seen so many police and we all just chatted until they were called away. One funny incident occurred when an Irish man asked a police man "Can you be'after telling me where the riot is?" "Yes," said the copper, "just go down this road, turn left, walk about a hundred yards, then turn right then second right and you're there." After he left us, I asked the copper, "Where have you sent him?" "God knows," he said.

Just after this we started to hear a lot of chanting followed by yelling and screaming and then all hell was let loose. First, we had to deal with a stream of injured police, mainly from bricks and bottles that were being thrown, then we started to get demonstrators with injuries. In the beginning they said they had been hit by the police (there were a lot of reporters there) but on examination quite a few appeared to have been hit by bricks thrown from the back of the demo that had failed to reach the police lines.

What had happened was a large group of demonstrators, some carrying coffins, were trying to storm Downing Street to get to Number 10. In those days there were no gates, or barrier as there is today. Also, another large group had gone onto Parliament Square and then to where we were stationed to try and get into Downing Street that way. Now, we were in the middle of a battle. One injured copper was brought in, who had been struck by one of the coffins that had been thrown at the police lines. He was quite surprised as he thought it was made of paper or balsa wood but it was not; it was a 100% genuine and it hurt. Then I saw a policeman on his own with truncheon drawn surrounded by five demonstrators all armed with pick-axe handles and was only saved by the intervention of six more police.

Eventually, at about ten o'clock it quietened down, we all had a cuppa, and tidied up the unit. I had never seen so many severe injuries. I think we treated over fifty cases that night.

On the way home Steve Smith and I got talking and he asked me if I would like to help train his competition team for the coming Area competitions as he had heard I was not bad at setting up sets and casualty make-up. What could I say? It was the start of my involvement with Airscrew Division.

The following day I saw in the News of the World a headline "Policeman draws his truncheon against peaceful demonstrators" and a picture. It was the incident that I had witnessed the night before, but they had cropped the picture so that it did not show the five guys. I was so disgusted that I stopped buying newspapers after that.

A short time later, an invitation was received by St John from Number 11 Downing Street for drinks in thanks of their work on that night. Our Superintendent's wife rang up and complained that she had not been invited and this caused a very embarrassing situation. She finally went, which really annoyed us as she had not even been on duty that night.

I was amazed at Airscrew Weybridge, with only ten members, but all so active, a training programme, lectures from all sorts of medical personnel, and one or two duties each week, (not like Addlestone's one or two a month).

Finally, in June, Steve spoke to me and said I had to make a decision either to go back to Addlestone or transfer to Airscrew as he would get into trouble about me. No contest. I transferred that June, in the year up to then I had attended four duties whilst at Addlestone. I attended sixteen more to the end of the year with Airscrew, so started my long association with them.

Airscrew Division was formed in May 1939 just prior to the outbreak of WWII as a closed works Division and registered as Airscrew, after the name of the company, Airscrew Howden who manufactured aircraft propellers. After the war the Division became open to anyone, meeting in the works social/sports club at the factory, which was located at Ham Court Industrial site. In 1949 the Cadet Division was formed.

Airscrew had the smallest area in the County (just one square mile) running from Addlestone station, down to the Basingstoke Canal and along to the River Wey. Because of this, County HQ altered the boundaries and changed the next Division, Weybridge & Walton to Walton & Oatlands, and Airscrew became Weybridge (Airscrew). This caused a lot of animosity from Walton members, which continued right up to when they closed down, believe it or not, in 2005.

 In 1969 the members had converted a redundant mobile display unit given to them by Airscrew Howden, into the Division's first

mobile first aid unit. County thought that it would be a big white elephant with no practical use. However, when London District heard about its existence, they requested it attended its first event, Trooping the Colour, closely followed by pop concerts, and demonstrations. The first real bloodying it got was the riot at the American Embassy in Grosvenor Square, where demonstrators tried to storm in. Shortly after this it was in action at the "Papa India" air crash at Staines.

The mobile unit had proved itself, and there was no looking back for LD 69, it's London District call sign, which would change many years later and become MD 627. The following year, 1970, the local Ambulance substation in Wey Road, Weybridge closed due to the opening of Ottershaw main station and the Division rented the premises from Surrey County Council and moved in.

Then in 1971, Steve Smith became the third Superintendent of the Division. Early in 1972, they took delivery of a brand new Ambulance; an Austin Morris JU250 van, with a Wadhams ambulance conversion -- total cost £2,000. When I transferred, the Division consisted of members Steve Smith and his wife Ann, Karen Palmer, Alice Phillips (Nursing Officer),Bob Hutton (Div Officer), Les Blake, Frank Staff, Jack Sleet, John Smith, Ron Bailey, Peter Tallant, with Jack Lenard (Div Treasurer), Phil Thomas (retired), and Dick Jones -- these latter three being non active.

2

THE MIDDLE YEARS (1973 – 1989)

On transferring, I was soon out on duty -- Chelsea football club, pop concerts, power boat racing, the Guildford show, scrambles, demos, Lord Mayor's Show, rugby at Twickenham and at the local rugby club.

One of the pop concerts that I attended was at the Oval and playing were "Hawkwind" and "Frank Zappa" -- a really odd person. Afterwards when it had finished, we were just checking around the ground and we came across a sleeping bag and I gave it a playful kick. This was followed by a yelp and the zip was pulled down and a girl and a man's head appeared rather bleary eyed, and asked "Has Frank Zappa been on yet?" They had slept through all that noise and they had bought tickets as well; what a waste.

But the funniest thing that happened to me this year was when we were on duty in November at the Lord Mayor's Show. On this particular day, a Saturday, we were supposed to cover the parade in the morning, and then at 12 o'clock leave to go onto Twickenham where New Zealand were playing England.

We were by St Paul's Cathedral and just before we were due to leave, we had a call to a building site were a brick had fallen some distance onto a brickie, landed on his hard hat, and caused quite a wound on his forehead where the hat had been rammed down. He was more interested in finishing his wall then being treated but eventually we persuaded him that he needed treatment, and of course we had to go to the nearest hospital. Now we were running late, and of course as we approached London Bridge we ran into a major traffic jam, so we were now crawling and a silly discussion occurred about whether or not, if we were to put on the blues and twos *[lights and sirens]* we could cross the bridge on the wrong side and get onto Twickenham, but it was decided that knowing our luck we would pick up a police escort and how would we explain that away; anyhow it was illegal.

Having moved a couple of metres, we stopped. Just then there was knocking on my window. I wound the window down and was asked by the young lady if this was the Ambulance she had called for. Explaining that we were not but with the congestion it probably would not be able to get through; I asked her what the problem was. She just said "Follow me", so I grabbed a kit and with a couple of our nurses, followed the girl into a boutique. Curled up on the floor with his hands in his crotch in a changing booth was her boyfriend. Blood was everywhere; on the floor, up the wall and all over a pair of white jeans. It transpired that he had been trying on a pair of jeans and had pulled up the zip without checking and had caught his manhood. On inspection I was horrified to see that it was nearly hanging off. As a bloke it makes your eyes water just to think about it, let alone see it, and then of course how do you dress it -- elevate the bleeding part above the heart? Grab it, lift it, dress it. In the end I gave him a dressing and told him to just press down on it.

The stretcher was brought in and he was loaded onto it and put into our ambulance. Now we could use our blues and twos, onto the wrong side of the road across the bridge and yes, of course, we picked up a police escort, onto St Thomas's Hospital (it was on the south side of the river). Result! Now to offload our casualty, and get on our way to Twickenham.

At St Thomas' A&E there was a well-known large West Indian Casualty Sister who was lovely, but did not suffer fools and idiots gladly, and unfortunately I had not thought what I was going to say on the handover. In we went with the patient and I then started with "male and er, he has, er, um, well, er," and at this she said "Come on St John, spit it out." Well that was me gone. Now laughing I managed to blurt out "He was trying on a pair of jeans..." She now guessed what the problem was, with "Is it right off?"

She then turned to the casualty, lifted the dressing, peered down at his crotch and said to him "Don't worry young man, we'll leave you with something to hold" at which point he fainted.

We made it to Twickenham by two thirty, but as usual England lost to the All Blacks. Months later we received a message via Les Blake, one of our members, who it turned out worked in the same large company in London as the young lady, thanking us for all the help, and that her boyfriend had recovered and everything was now in FULL working order.

****

I had always been of the mind that we (St John Ambulance) did not sell ourselves to the local community. We did all this good work but the general public had no idea what we did, so one evening I spoke to Steve and Bob Hutton about using the local press and was told, "You can give it a go, but you are wasting your time, as we have tried before." Little did they know where it would lead.

Though it was against regulations to take pictures while on duty, from thereon in I always carried a camera with me, but only to take pictures of St John in action, with pictures telling a story and not just members standing to attention by an ambulance. In fact one day the commissioner of London ran up to me and asked me to take some pictures for him. I said "You know we are not allowed to carry a camera with us." He just said "Don't be silly, we all know that you always have one. Just bring it with you".

In November of this year whilst on the way to a scramble at Pirbright, the mobile unit was involved in a head-on crash when a car came across the road. This led to the unit being repaired and resprayed all white (now really the big white elephant).

1973 saw my long suffering wife joining, as "if you can't beat them, join them." Also, the children were now old enough to be left with the grandparents.

In May, I saw one of the best concerts that I have ever seen. We were requested to cover with London District, a pop concert at Earls Court. On asking who was playing we were told it was Pink Floyd. I'd never heard of them, so I asked one of the security men there what were they like, and he said they were not his type of music but the stage show was unbelievable, and the flying bomb was some thing to see. Flying bomb! My mind went into overdrive.

The show started. Wow, what a show -- "Dark Side of the Moon" -- all those tunes that are now classic, "Money", "Time and Us" and "Them." It was the first time I had ever seen a story as a pop concert, and the group were just dressed in normal clothes. I was so hooked that the following week I bought the LP (record) and it's been one of my favourites since. Incidentally I had the luck to see them again in 1995 at the now O2 Arena; they were older, greyer and fatter, but they still filled the venue with fans and the music was just as good.

Some one told us that the regional competitions were to be held in Guernsey this year, so we entered a team, won the Area competitions (comps), and came second in the County comps only to learn that it was not in Guernsey, but Bognor, great! Think we got conned.

We also had two members join us for nine months from St John in Australia; Joy and Warren Burgess with their three children. Warren was here in England to study for both the National Ambulance Service and St John Ambulance. Our ladies and female Cadets were quite jealous of Joy and her daughter's white uniform, and Joy's hat. We (the men) weren't as keen on Warren's as his summer uniform was shorts, but it was very interesting to learn about St John in Australia.

In July, Weybridge (Airscrew) received the County Colour (this is dedicated to the memory of past members of St John), and is handed to a Division for safekeeping for a year, and involves a Colour Ceremony and memorial service plus a parade. As none of us had any training in marching as a Colour Party we went to the army at Keogh Barracks to get some training. The only problem was that one of us marched, as the Drill Sergeant said, like a clockwork orange, i.e. right arm and right leg together; try marching behind someone like that! Thank goodness he was not available to be in the Colour Party when we paraded the Colour through Weybridge in September, when it was laid up in St James Church.

I don't know why, but I seem to attract trouble. On the way back in the ambulance from Runnymede Pleasure Park in August, as we were just coming down Chertsey Road, I noticed a horse and rider on the opposite side of the road having trouble with her mount, so I slowed down. Unfortunately, a car towing a caravan coming the other way did not and tried to overtake them. This caused the horse to throw off the rider. The horse then crashed into the caravan. I had not realised how fragile a caravan was; the whole thing just exploded and the horse fell to the ground. Luckily the rider was not injured, but the horse was not so lucky. By this time it had managed to get up on its feet, but looked like it had broken its jaw and had a few cuts on its body; how do you treat that?

But the best was the woman passenger of the car. She went mad, screaming at the rider, blaming her for the accident and why did she not keep control of the horse, and what were they going to do as they were on there way to the New Forest for the week's holiday;. Not once did she ask how the rider or horse was. Once the police arrived, after giving my details, we went on our way.

The whole of the year was taken up with rugby both at Twickenham and our local club, the Easter parade in Battersea Park, Trooping the Colour and lots of demonstrations in London. The Commissioner of London District was Mr Derek Fenton and sometimes we would receive a phone call from him on Saturday morning at ten o'clock with the request "We need your mobile unit at such and such Embassy by 1300 hours," and we went; in fact we ended up being referred to as "Fenton's Marauders" as we seemed to maraud all over London, and knew the location of nearly every Embassy in London,. He was the sort of leader that you would follow anywhere.

We attended yet another pop concert at Earls Court, this time the Osmonds with lots of screaming teeny-boppers, with us treating many suffering from hyperventilation. Another first for us was the Royal Wedding of Princess Anne in November, and we ended the year with what would become a regular duty -- seeing the New Year in at Trafalgar Square and treating revellers that had got injured.

****

1974 saw the Australians (Warren and family) returning home, and again competitions with the Division getting through to the regional finals again, along with all the usual duties.

The most notorious one happened after the Division had been at the Trooping of the Colour when a request was made for any unit available to stay and cover a demo at Red Lion Square involving a march by the National Front. A clash between the Front and anti- Front supporters resulted in our members dealing with a semi-conscious student that was taken to hospital and later died. This resulted in the members who treated him having to go to the inquest and give statements.

One of the St John courses opened to us was an Air Attendant course; the idea was when qualified you could escort injured holiday makers back to the UK, though you could be sent anywhere in the world at a moments notice, and the practicality of being able to drop everything and

go was debatable. Still it gave nine of us a chance to try an emergency chute out of an aeroplane -- that was fun -- and also a flight in an unpressurised aircraft to get some practical experience. The latter involved us getting up early one morning and driving up to a RAF flight training station in Cambridge.

This would have been alright but I had been to a stag night the night before and was feeling a bit worse for wear (hangover). The first problem was that the RAF did not have a flying suit small enough to fit my wife as she was only four foot, eleven inches high, then when she tried on the parachute she nearly fell over backwards with the weight of it. Then a shock -- parachute training normally takes two weeks but we were going to get five minutes. Basically, if anything goes wrong, follow the pilot. Nice – any questions? I asked did you have to yell "Geronimo" when leaving the aeroplane. I was told, "Yell what you like!"

Now the next shock, walking out to the aircraft, we walked past all the modern planes to a old twin engine Vickers Varsity built in the 1950's; still at least it had been built at Weybridge. The pilot informed us that they called them "flying pigs." So there we were, kitted up with suit, helmet, parachute, emergency parachute and, thank goodness, a sick bag each. Off we went. The idea was to fly up to three thousand feet and experience air pressure, then the pilot had to practice landings and taking off from an abandoned airfield. This in fact involved just touching down and bouncing up in the air many, many times. This led to me using my sick bag, then Kate's, the pilot's, navigator's and the radio operator's. I have never felt so ill for such a long time, yet as soon as we landed and I touched the ground, the sickness went and I was starving and went straight to the NAAFI where I had a full English breakfast.

We even got lost while up in the air and rather then asking control for our location the pilot flew low over a motorway while we looked for junction numbers before returning back to base.

Have you noticed how good we are at diagnosing casualties but when it comes down to us and the family something goes wrong? Sam, our daughter had an accident while playing with her little brother in the woods, and broke her wrist. They should have not been there playing so they did not tell us, and we did not even notice that she was using her right hand rather then her left, though she was left handed. It was a fortnight later when she was with us at a scramble at Pirbright, she fell over and returned to the mobile unit in tears, and even then we did not take it seriously until our Nursing Officer checked her out. When she made Sam hold up her arm it was the classic dinner fork fracture. She still reminds me about it thirty years later.

Apart from that, 1974 was a good year for recruitment; at the end of the year the membership had increased to 29.

Finally in April 1975, we made it to Guernsey for the regional competitions. We left by ship on Friday from Weymouth, and on the way, one of the team suffered sea sickness, probably not helped by Ron Bailey and myself eating bacon, eggs and sausages in front of him. Still, it was quite interesting watching him change colour before he did a runner to the toilets. The competition was held on the Saturday afternoon and we came third, scoring 245 points, just one behind the second place (246), and only two behind the winning team (247). If only one of us had made a neck collar up from a news paper, we would have got an extra ten marks. Still that's what competitions are all about; a little bit of luck.

We had a wonderful time in Guernsey. We stayed with a St John member at his home; a bungalow on the outskirts of St Peter Port and after returning from the dinner and dance we all went to bed ready to return back home the following day. About two thirty in the morning there was a knock on our window. Ron had gone to the toilet and snapped the key off in the lock, locking himself in. He then had to crawl out of a very small window before waking us up; nice P.Js though.

So it was back to Weybridge and waiting for us were more duties, the first being three evenings at Earls Court, for the rock group Led Zeppelin. Up to now, apart from Pink Floyd, most concerts consisted of a warm up group, usually not that good but not always, then a long break, before the main group played for about an hour.

Arriving at Earls Court straight from work, we soon had the fans arriving, nearly all in black leather jackets, greasy jeans, motor bike helmets, beards and tattoos. Apart from the girls, it looked like a Hell's Angels convention.

One guy walked up to me and said "'Ere St John" and I was rather worried what he was about to say. I answered "Yes Sir" and with a big beaming smile he said "Thanks mate for all the good work you guys do, one of you saved my mate's life in a road accident." I learned something very important that evening -- don't judge people by their dress or colour.

As for the concert, at eight o'clock the curtain went up and there they were in all their glory, dressed in jeans and casual tops. What a concert, from "Whole Lotta Love" and "Stairway to Heaven" to "Dazed and Confused"; the place rocked. I don't remember an interval and at the end there was an encore that lasted 30 minutes. Three hours of solid rock. The only injury I treated all night was a police officer who got an ear plug stuck in his ear. The air was full of sweet smelling smoke from the cigarettes that were being smoked by the audience and Led Zep.

It was interesting that the Ambulance seemed to glide home back to Weybridge, and my wife made me hang my uniform in our garage because of the nice sweet smell it had picked up. Since then I have been a massive fan of Led Zep. I've even got slight hearing damage put down to many loud concerts attended; still it was worth it.

From this it was all downhill, with us going to the Odeon Hammersmith for the Bay City Rollers concerts, one on Friday evening followed by two on Saturday. What a difference -- late starting, grotty first group, an hour before they appeared on stage, and then they played the eight songs they knew and that was it. Oh sorry, I forgot to mention about the three thousand hysterical screaming young female fans, some aged only nine or ten. On the first night we treated over a hundred and twenty. We got kicked, punched and scratched as we tried to treat them; some had to be taken to hospital for suspected fractured ribs and others needed further treatment for hysteria.

Earlier in the month I had invited a newspaper reporter Mrs Pat Cole from the local "Review" to join us on a duty to see what we did, and it so happened that she had arranged with us to come out on the Saturday. After the previous night we were now wearing shin pads to protect our legs, and some of us had managed to borrow cricket boxes; that's how bad it had been the night before. We also had a large supply of airline sick bags.

One of the major flash points was at the front of the

stage, there was an orchestra pit underneath it, and the fans were climbing over each other to get to the group but would fall 5ft into the pit. Two stretcher parties were now stationed there and just like the night before, the fans were kept waiting until they were hyped up. The group came on and all hell broke loose; there we were trying to catch the kids as they fell down on top of us as a few got knocked out when they hit their heads on some of the iron supports. All this in semi-darkness, the audience screaming, and the band playing.

We then started to have broken seats thrown at us; at this stage the concert was halted temporarily so we could move the injured out. One of the casualties I dealt with was unconscious, and having loaded her onto a stretcher I yelled to some one in uniform "Don't just stand there, get hold of the stretcher and help us to get her outside." It was not until we got outside that I saw it was Derek Fenton, District Commissioner. Ooops! He just smiled at me and then went back to help. That evening the sick bags were used in synchronised breathing; we had groups of fifteen to twenty girls all hyperventilating. They all had a bag each to breathe in and out of, with one of us giving the instructions, "Everybody breathe in, now everyone breathe out" -- it worked though! Our poor reporter, who I had been trying to look after had tried to follow us in to the concert and ended up being manhandled by a couple of stewards, even after she explained that she was just covering St John in action. They then tried to get her camera off her as they did not want any pictures being taken, but she managed to keep it. All told we treated a hundred and eighty three that day with thirty four being sent to hospital including a security man with a suspected fractured leg. The net result of taking a reporter with us was a full page story with pictures in our local paper, and she even wrote an article for our national magazine, the St John Review. What a result!

The rest of the year was taken up with all the usual events -- fetes, rugby matches and pop concerts. The pop concerts included Queen, Mud, Eton John, David Bowie, Genesis and the Rolling Stones to name just a few, they are the perks of being in St John. We finished the year with the usual Boxing Day Scramble and New Year's Eve (NYE) at Trafalgar Square.

****

1976 turned out to be a year to remember. Earlier in the year, two local lads had drowned when their car had crashed into the Thames on the river road in Shepperton. This, and an article in the St John Review on the safety boat run by Reading Division made us think about our needs in the area, especially with Weybridge being surrounded by the Thames and the River Wey. The Division decided to purchase a boat and equipment, and that's how MD901 (response boat call sign) came into being. As usual we had no funds, but still purchased the boat/engine and trailer anyway, now to raise the money -- £800 plus another £300/£400 for equipment. Airscrew Howden organised a charity walk, which raised over £700 and with other fund raising events and donations the rest was soon reached. Now we have the boat, now comes the training.

As there were no regulations, we set about researching what other water rescue organisations used. First – swimming. It was decided that we all would need bronze in personal survival, though swimming in our pyjamas for four lengths of a swimming pool, and saving a brick from the bottom, did not seem relevant, but still we did it. As luck would have it, two of the members owned and sailed dinghies so we could practice "man overboard!" Some of us even got to try sailing and one Sunday we went to Stokes Bay in the Solent. This would help us understand where and why we needed to position our boat if helping a dinghy in trouble. True to form I was the one who got a smack in the face from a boom, and also managed to crack a couple of ribs when slipping over on the seaweed.

I came home with a lovely black eye and learnt how to advise anyone with cracked ribs what not to do, i.e. don't cough, sneeze or laugh 'cos it hurts!

At the same time London District was also setting up a boat section though it was staffed by members from other Divisions and their boats were Rigid Inflatable Boats (RIBs) because of the tidal nature of the Thames. While this was going on we were still attending our usual events, but a new one was the Cup Final in May at Wembley; not in the stadium but just outside at the entrance. We were quite busy, treating over sixty casualties. It was Manchester United playing against Southampton and Southampton won.

In June at the Trooping of the Colour, two of the guys, Pete Tallent and Jack Sleet had decided to have a laugh and present me with a mock medal, as I was doing so many duties and also appearing in the press (could they have been jealous?) Steve Smith was not too amused as they did it in front of the Commissioner; still I had the last laugh with what happened next year by the time of the Trooping of the Colour.

Having such a result with the press at the Bay City Rollers concert the year before, I thought I would try again with a reporter from the local Surrey Herald, so I invited him to one of the six Rolling Stones concerts we were covering at Earls Court. This time not so lucky; a very quiet evening apart from the music -- can't win them all! Still isn't it funny how fate can help you? Just as we were getting home we came across a road traffic accident at Shepperton; a car on its roof with an injured driver -- yet another good press report in the paper.

1976 saw another first for us; a "board of enquiry." This occurred after we had someone transferred from London District in 1975. We were warned the he was a bit of a barrack room lawyer (knows the regulations back to front) and a couple of our female members felt that there was something not right with him but its not easy to refuse when he is already in St John. Anyhow, he joined and did not step out of line and did his fair share of the duties. One thing he did do though was when my daughter, now age seven showed him her wobbly tooth, he just grabbed it and pulled it out; neither she nor I were very amused.

But it was not until we were on duty at the Bay City Rollers that his actions caused trouble. While I was doing the synchronised breathing trick, he appeared with a Rollers scarf and started to wave it in front of them, causing them to hyperventilate again. I told him to stop it. He then got very cross with me and it ended with me threatening to hit him, and by nature I am not a violent person.

Then at the riots at Notting Hill, I was treating a woman police officer who had been hit on her boob by a brick and was in a lot of pain. Although it would have been better for a female to treat her, it was not practical so I was holding a cold compress on her chest whilst waiting for an ambulance. Afterwards he came up and said with a smirk "I bet you enjoyed doing that" and at first I could not understand what he was on about; as far as I was concerned she was a casualty, but he then started to make rude remarks and again we exchanged a few heated words.

Shortly after this incident he finally went too far. When at the Stones concert at Earls Court, he grabbed a fan who was running towards the stage causing her to spin round and hit her head on a metal pillar knocking her out. This happened in front of a London District Staff Officer who, when challenging him on his action, received a lot a verbal abuse resulting in him being ordered off the duty. The Officer concerned was a good friend of Weybridge and asked if we (Surrey) could deal with this incident rather then London District getting involved. After the inquiry he was given a choice; resign from St John or face a civil action for assault. He resigned.

Many years later his name appeared in our local newspaper. He had been charged and found guilty of molesting young girls and it was also reported that he had been discharged from the RAF for similar problems. Now today, I hope with CRB checks this should not happen

It was a well accepted fact that if a demo occurred on a Sunday it was nearly always quiet with only a few casualties; on the other hand if it was held on a Saturday or a Bank Holiday Monday it seemed to have the potential to be very hectic. Whether this was anything to do with the Sunday drinking laws, (pubs opened at midday and shut at two in the afternoon, remaining shut until seven, when they re-opened) -- I don't know.

One of these Sunday demos was the Anti-Apartheid march from the South African Embassy by Trafalgar Square to Hyde Park. We started at the Embassy, then as the march left, went onto Hyde Park. It was a very hot and sunny day and as the march arrived, the police, wearing full uniform that had been marshalling it broke away, their job done. One of their Superintendents came over to us and asked if we had anything his men could drink as no-one had arranged anything for them. On board our mobile unit we carried about twenty gallons of water so we started to give his men a drink. The next we knew, there was a massive long line of police all waiting for a drink, and then one of them asked laughingly if there was any chance of some ice. Well, we had a block of

ice on board too, so there we were breaking up the ice with a hammer and a screwdriver, and the reputation of Weybridge St John was established with the Met Police.

Two men dressed in jeans and anoraks looking like demonstrators went and joined the line and I heard a couple of police telling them to push off as it was for them. They turned round and said "Look mate, we are Special Branch and have been in the march and yelling for the last two hours." They got a drink. A month later we learnt that some one had written into the Job (the police magazine) a letter asking how come St John Ambulance could supply them with drinks, yet their own catering unit failed to even turn up. Shortly after this article we had a phone call from the Met catering unit asking us if we made a habit of feeding the police when on duty with them. We told them yes, if the situation allowed, from the Commissioner downwards, why? They then told us that next time we were in London to let them know and they would give us a supply of tea, coffee, sugar and cups, and let them know if we needed anything else.

****

The Division had been booked for the first time to attend the annual two-day Notting Hill Carnival on the August bank holiday weekend. Both Steve and Bob were away for the weekend, so it was left to me to drive the mobile with a crew of four, including Kate, my wife, to Notting Hill and run the station. Not knowing much about the Carnival we went into the duty naively thinking that it was just a parade followed by a party, though I quite like Bob Marley and Reggae music. We were stationed at Oxford Gardens which is at the top end of Portobello Road, just the north side of the West Way and midway between Ladbroke Grove and All Saints Road, and were one of three mobile first aid units deployed in the area for the day. I had never seen so many West Indians, and a passing car stopped and the driver, a white guy, said to me, "We are the bloody foreigners here mate." Nice start to the duty!

Sunday, as usual, turned out to be relatively quiet, with us treating twenty three casualties, mainly assaults with a couple of stabbings. With some London District members from another station we were taken out by the police and fed at a rest area in the afternoon. Eventually we were stood down at eleven p.m., but you could feel the undertones that evening.

The following day we departed from Weybridge at nine a.m. to be on station by ten with a fresh crew. Unfortunately, we could not get babysitters for the Monday so my wife had to stay at home. Due to the estimated two hundred and fifty thousand crowd expected, three extra first aid stations were deployed with a total of eight St John Ambulances. Everything remained quiet with just a few casualties being treated, so mid-afternoon three of us from our station went for a meal break with the police. On returning in a police van, the driver informed us that he could not get us back to our station, so he would drop us as near as he could. Great! Where did he drop us? Just by the "Elgin Pub." It then dawned on me I had left my white haversack and hat back on the unit. I looked just like a policeman. Looking up Ladbroke Grove, it was heaving, and the way people were looking at me, I decided maybe that was not an option. So making sure that the nurse (Silvia Berrett) who was with me stayed close, we managed to get up to Portobello Road and then onto our station. Though I did not tell her, I felt very scared for the first time in my life. It was just 4:30 p.m. when we got back to the unit and then all hell broke loose, police running everywhere, and within a few minutes, police casualties were being brought back to us with injuries from bricks and bottles that had been thrown at them, then some with stab wounds, others who had been beaten up etc.

Then we started to receive injured public, some who also with stab wounds. Earlier we had been supplied with a doctor from London District for our station, but it turned out he was a psychiatrist, complete with the grey beard and fag ash or dandruff over the front of his uniform, plus he spoke with a foreign accent. Not what you want on a unit during a riot; all he was interested in was psychoanalysing the casualties on their feelings about what had happened to them.

We were now inundated with casualties. At one stage I was treating a police officer with a serious wound to the head while getting him to put pressure on a colleague's arm that had a knife wound. Suddenly a gentleman appeared on the unit in civilian clothes. I asked him what he was doing here, as sometimes you could get reporters trying to get a story for the papers. He informed me he was a doctor, but being of a suspicious mind I asked him to prove it. Oh boy! He was a London District surgeon, plus medical officer for Wormwood Scrubs prison, and then said to me, a lowly ambulance member "What do you want me to do?" "Prioritise the casualties please," I requested as we were all so busy that it was not being done.

We had been now continually treating for three hours when the generator suddenly stopped. A quick check showed that we had run out of fuel. Wondering where I was going to get petrol in the middle of all this, a police officer asked me what the problem was. I explained, and he said, "Well you won't get any petrol around here but are you any good siphoning petrol out of a car?" Is the Pope Catholic? I work in the motor trade. So he said, "See that car parked near the unit, it's an unmarked police car and if you have some tubing, you have got petrol. There we were busy siphoning away when he started to smile. When I ask him what's up, he said "If someone throws a petrol bomb, you and me have had it, and I'd love to see the driver of this car when he comes back and sees that his petrol's disappeared."

Next problem, running low on water, solution -- near us was a Convent. I knocked on the door and a nun opened the little flap. I explained I required some water and she let me in -- what a change. It was so quiet and peaceful compared to outside, I was nearly tempted to stay there. As I was leaving with the water, one of the nuns said, "Sounds like they are really enjoying the Carnival." I didn't have the heart to tell her the truth. It was back to reality, more injured police to treat. At this time all the police had to defend themselves were their truncheons, so they improvised with dustbin lids and empty milk crates to protect them selves against missiles being thrown at them. One semi-conscious police officer was brought to us on a stretcher still clutching a dustbin lid and when he arrived at our station his colleagues were trying to prise it out of his hands; that's how short they were of dustbin lids.

While all this was going on we were organising the retuning ambulances to pick up food for the police as a lot of them had not eaten since breakfast. It was somewhat surreal as at the rear of the unit we were treating and at

the front we were feeding the police with meat pies and cups of tea. At about ten o'clock it started to quieten down and someone said that we better let our other halves know that we were all right (don't forget we did not have mobile phones in those days), so we all queued up by a nearby phone box and it was only when I spoke to Kate that I realised how dangerous it had been, and that it was being reported that it was a race riot with ambulances and police cars being attacked.

We were finally stood down at midnight. As we left a large group of police who were resting suddenly gave us a cheer and yelled "Thanks St John." That made it all worth it. I can still remember the sound of crunching glass as we drove over all the broken bottles that lay on the road. We finally got back to Weybridge at one thirty in the morning. We had treated over a hundred and thirty cases and forty four had been taken to hospital from our station. We also brought back a memento of that day -- a broken truncheon. The overall total for Monday was three hundred and eighty six treated and a hundred and fourteen admitted to hospital, and we had been on duty for over sixteen hours. Seven hours later at work, I started to receive phone calls telling me that my picture was in the national press, from the Sun to the Daily Telegraph. Even my dad rang me to tell me with the remark "You look terrible." I'm not surprised having been on duty for thirty hours in the last forty-eight.

So it was back to normal duties to the end of the year, though we attended a free pop concert in Hyde Park, and still ended up treating a hundred and forty three casualties, and again the Bay City Rollers at the New Victoria Theatre -- sixty more teeny boppers treated. In October, the safety boat was inspected by Princess Anne at Sandhurst while on display at the National Cadet Rally. Also later in the month, we found a replacement for our mobile unit as it was beginning to show its age. The new unit was a Bedford coach, which had been converted into a display unit for a damp-proofing company. It was parked in a railway station car park, and was going to cost us £550.

That was going to be our project for 1977 which was also going to be the Queen's Jubilee year with all the special events that it would bring.

****

1977 started our long association with the film and TV media. Weybridge had been chosen to appear in a documentary film by EMI to be released later to cinemas throughout the country, and it would feature the boat involved in a water rescue and members on duty at a motor bike scramble. Our boat that had started life as "Sierra Juliet 88" and was signed as "First Aid Rescue" had now been renamed "St John Ambulance 7" for legal reasons. The filming was on the lake at Thorpe Park. I had conned a work colleague, Paul Charles, to volunteer to be the person in the water, this being on a very cold Sunday in February. Poor old Paul; the sequence would only be about five minutes in the twenty minute film but it took from eleven in the morning till about three in the afternoon. By the end, he was starting to get hypothermia. I don't think he ever trusted me again.

As it was a first, I could not miss an opportunity to get press coverage so had a reporter cover the filming -- yet another good article in the local Surrey Herald. Two weeks later we were at Pirbright filming the second part while still covering the actual event. We must have loaded the "casualty" on and off our Land Rover ten times. All you would get was "Great, but can we try that again?" from the producer; never did see the film though.

As we had been to Guernsey last year, we thought we had better enter the Area Competitions this year, so it did not look as if we had only entered for the trip (well we did really). Unfortunately we won, even though we'd walked onto the set with no competition training, and been debating who the team leader would be. We were told by one judge that as a team we were four very good individuals, so with all the duties and the work on the new unit we tried not to win or come second in the County round. We nearly slipped up; if it had not been for someone putting the wrong arm in a sling we might have finished first. He maintained that he did it on purpose anyhow.

Between March and May, Bob Hutton had been very busy finding companies to cut out the rear of our new mobile unit and put in an access and also to convert the inside to something that didn't look like a junk yard. Also, the members had meetings about what they would like in the unit and a plan was drawn up. In May we had an unexpected royal visitor when HRH Princess Margaret, while inspecting a parade, showed interest in the mobile unit and chatted informally to some of us.

One day, while at work, I received a phone call from my wife saying that I had a letter from the Prime Minister. Well, as you don't normally receive letters like that, and after what happened with the mock medal last year, I thought that the boys might be doing another wind up, especially as I had been asked to become the Divisional Transport Officer. I asked Kate if it looked genuine and she said yes, and that it had "Her Majesty's Service" on it. So I said, "Well you'd better open it, might be a tax bill." It all went very quiet followed by "BLOODY HELL!" She then said, "You have been awarded the British Empire Medal for Notting Hill last year, but you are not allowed to tell anyone until after it comes out in the Queens

Birthday Honours list in June." Stunned and gobsmacked, I thought "Why me? I was only doing my job." Then it sank in that I'd been awarded the BEM. A civilian award and I'm only an Ambulance member, wow. Then I thought of Peter and Jack and what happened last year; how ironic.

We were hoping to have the new mobile (Mk II) up and running for the Trooping the Colour so that any teething problems could be ironed out before Notting Hill, but the conversion took longer then expected; the cutting out and strengthening of the rear end for the doors causing the delay. What an improvement though; four treatment beds instead of two, a seated treatment area, surgery bay, a kitchen area with a Calor gas ring for tea, coffee and soup and a radio room. Outside at the rear, on the roof, we had mounted a pod that when needed at night could be raised up eight foot and it contained four arc lights that lit up the surrounding area. On the downside, it was thirty eight foot long, had a lot of glass in the roof, which

on a hot sunny day made it like being in a greenhouse, and on a very wet day it could spring leaks. Driving was fun as it was addicted to Easystart; this was a spray you used to start some diesels on very cold days by spraying a jet of it into the air cleaner. Mk II needed this no matter what the weather was like. On the plus side though, it had power steering and a five speed gear box. Though the old Mk I was only thirty foot in length, it had no power steering, which meant that if trying to do a three/five point turn, it took two of you to turn the steering wheel. It also only had a three speed crash gear box, which meant you had to double de-clutch every time you changed gear.

After driving it to London and back, your left leg and both arms certainly knew it. Mk II was a vast improvement and you felt like you were driving a Rolls Royce, but because of the size of Mk II we had to find somewhere else to park it. Firstly, at Airscrew, and after a lot of negotiations by Bob Hutton, we were given permission to park it by British Aerospace at Brooklands airfield, and there it stayed when not on duty for the next eight years, acquiring a resident -- a mouse. We never saw it, but we knew it was on board by the teeth marks in the soap, and through finding a nest in a sterile dressing.

The old Mk I was sold on to Ipswich Division, and Mk II became operational on August 14th. The first duty instead of a quiet one turned out to be a baptism of fire, with us covering the National Front march in Lewisham. This time I stayed at home while my wife went on duty; the unit one of three deployed for the event which turned very violent with a series of running battles of considerable intensity with smoke bombs, bricks, missiles including for the first time ammonia bombs being thrown. Over a hundred casualties were treated, one being a Sun newspaper reporter who had been mugged, losing all his cameras and requiring hospital treatment.

The members arrived back at Weybridge with a list of minor modifications to be done before Notting Hill in less than two weeks time; still with two or three evenings work everything was ready. After the experiences of last year's Carnival things were changed, the police now had riot shields; very heavy and about five foot in length. Also feeding arrangements were well organised with us and the police were taken to a tented area at Perk's Field, much earlier in the day for a three course meal and given a packed lunch box to eat at teatime.

I did think it was a bit odd though, that the police had a tent with films showing to the police on reserve, these being Dirty Harry and Zulu; someone had a warped sense of humour. True to form Sunday was quiet, with only a small number of casualties, but Monday turned sour in the evening with muggings and stabbings, and when the police moved in, violent clashes occurred. I don't know whether it was the films they had watched earlier, but when a shield unit went into action you could hear them banging the shields with their truncheons in a regular beat, just like the Zulus. One of those mugged that we treated was the same Sun reporter that we had treated at Lewisham, though this time not so badly injured and we (St John) had a really good write up in the newspaper next day.

As far as power for the unit, someone told us that there would be a power socket run of a lamp post at our station. True to form, when we arrived there was nothing, but undeterred I worked out how to wire into a lamp post, and while I was doing this I looked up to see a policeman standing over me, who asked me if I knew that it constituted theft. I pointed out that without power we would not be able to treat people in the dark and also we would not be able to supply tea and coffee for the police, so we came to an understanding.

That year, I managed to crew an ambulance at Notting Hill, instead of staying on the unit all day. One of the calls was interesting. A police officer had seen a man fall off one of the lorries that drove around the carnival route carrying the   playing steel band. On arrival he told us that the man had only fallen about three feet but there was something wrong with him; he was either drunk and or had been taking drugs. We asked him his name but all we got from him was Augustus Barnet and as we were outside a wine shop of the same name we decided that was not correct. When we asked for an address, we got London Transport, from a parked bus. Then he kept going blank and wasn't responsive. He was placed inside our ambulance and was given a top to toe check but we could not find any reason for this and decided to take him to hospital. As we arrived at St Mary's and were handing over to a London Ambulance Service (LAS) officer, I just checked the casualty again and now saw a trickle of fluid from his ear; fractured base of skull? He died two days later from a cerebral haemorrhage but it was nearly six months later before they found out his details.

It was back to all our regular duties, apart from October when we received a request for us to cover a National Front march in, of all places, Manchester. So off we went up there. It turned out to be a total waste of time and we only treated one casualty. The end of the year saw our usual events finishing of with us treating fifty two casualties in Trafalgar Square. One of these made us smile. A man riding on a back of a car fell off, smashed his mouth and knocked out a few teeth, and it so happened that our nurse was a dental nurse who gave him an in-depth diagnosis and possible treatment on the way to hospital; really cheered him up, (NOT). Our floodlight on the unit proved itself every useful in lighting up an area next to us where we could leave our drunks to recover; this soon got named "the drunk pen."

****

Until I joined Weybridge, I had never seen a rugby match, let alone understood what it was all about, but one of the main local duties we attended all through the winter months was Vandals Rugby Club near Walton Bridge with five pitches. In fact I was told that before we had an ambulance, the Divisional members used to cycle to the club to cover the matches. I soon learned that, to quote Oscar Wilde -- football was a game for gentlemen played by hooligans, while rugby was a game for hooligans played by gentlemen. I personally think it is a game designed to give St John members the chance to practice their first aid skills. Where else could you treat broken arms and legs, see dislocations, cuts on heads, teeth knocked out, cracked ribs and concussion all in one afternoon? I joke, but sometimes it felt like it was like that; who could fail to remember the sound of a breaking leg on a cold December afternoon followed by the "golly gosh St John I think I've hurt myself?" If you believe that you will believe anything. The wonderful thing about rugby was that the referee was totally in charge; no one argued with them and if you did you lost ten yards. The players were so grateful with us being there. We also covered the international matches and the Five Nations competitions at Twickenham. Some of my best experiences occurred when the French played there. They always had a village band that played all through the match, and there was always a smuggled cockerel brought in, usually painted in red, white and blue paint, so when they played at Twickenham, there was always a member from the RSPCA to deal with any animals.

One match, the RSPCA man walked up to us with a very unwell bird in his arms saying it looked like it would not survive, so the police officer who was with us just took it and wrung its neck. The poor RSPCA man just stood with his mouth open -- stunned.

Another time we lost a stretcher, but it was found at the end of the match. Two Frenchmen were carrying a semi-conscious drunken friend on it to the underground station, and how they were going to get him onto a train, we had no idea. But I supposed the funniest incident was when we were called to the men's toilets by the police when it appeared that a Frenchman had gone to the toilet and not come out. He had, in fact, collapsed in one of the cubicles. After a lot of shouting and banging on the door which got no response, the police officer decided to kick the door in. Unfortunately, it turned out that our man had passed out and his head was resting against the door and our helpful policeman had just added to his problems. We had with us a young and enthusiastic member for who this was his first duty and he volunteered to go over the top of the cubical which had a small gap. Unfortunately, he slipped and fell, putting his foot into the toilet pan and trying to save himself grabbed the chain, flushing his foot. As you can imagine by now we were all in hysterics. Anyhow, we got the man out, who was then taken to hospital.

The great thing about rugby fans was they were so friendly with each other, the police and us; not like the football fans we had come across. Our local Vandals rugby duties finally came to a close in the mid-nineties due to them being no longer willing to pay for our services, and the club forgetting to inform us when matches changed times and even days. It would five years though before we would start covering rugby again. (In 2003 Walton & Oatlands Division was finally closed and Weybridge inherited their area which included Esher Rugby Club. A request was received from them for first aid cover, both on Saturdays and Sundays. We were back to the first aid I love doing).

In April 1977, I received my BEM, and though I hoped it would be from the Queen, I received a letter from Her Majesty stating that she could not present it to me personally due to work commitments so it would be presented by the County Sherriff at County Hall at Kingston. Still the whole family went to see me receive it from Lord Hamilton of Dalzell.

****

1978. February saw our first involvement with sailing clubs with our safety boat. We had come to the conclusion that the chance of us being on the water at the right time and the right place was very remote. Therefore we had looked at where our services would be needed and of course sailing clubs needed safety boats, and with the added bonus of trained first aiders on board, we fitted the bill. Our first event was at Staines Sailing club and we received a letter from them stating how very impressed they were with us. Having created such a good impression, we were asked to attend a British Olympic Yachting Appeal pro/celebrity sailing event to be held at the Queen Mary Sailing club at Ashford. This started a long association with the club covering many of their major events.

Also in February a new member joined -- Virginia Johnson (Ginny) who was to become a great friend.

Ginny was a typical Weybridge (the town) person; frightfully well spoken, and willing to take anyone on who she thought needed taking down a peg or two. Once on a quiet demo, we were attempting to do the Telegraph crossword and we had got stuck on a word. Ginny, seeing a police Sergeant, called him over and said "Sergeant chappie, you must be brainy to be a Sergeant. Is there such a thing as scrum pox?" Amazingly he knew there was; it was an infection you could get on the shoulder when playing rugby.

Another time a rather aggressive security guard at a local duty started on her with "Oy love, you can't leave your bleeding car there. Move it." Ginny explained that she was not his love and the car was not bleeding and after she had finished with him he went and parked her car for her, and was calling her Madam. Only Ginny! She became my Divisional Officer in 1986 and finally left St John in 1999.

In April, our friends the National Front started up again with a march through Brixton, but this passed off without too much trouble. Yet more firsts -- attending

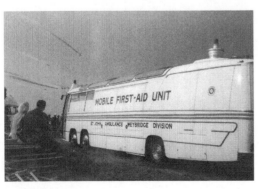

Derby Day at Epsom , and the International Air Fair at Biggin Hill, which although in Kent, came under London District, and as aircraft are one of my other loves, I was in my element seeing all the flying that took place over the two days.

Having attended yet another pop concert at Earls Court, Bob Dylan, (who I thought was a good songwriter but as a singer left a lot to be desired), we then found ourselves on duty at an open air concert the following week at Blackbush aerodrome with him as the main attraction. What a difference a venue makes; at Earls Court we treated about twenty casualties, while at Blackbush we were on duty for over eighteen hours and treated four hundred and seventy-six. Needless to say this was on a Saturday.

The next day found us at Brick Lane in the East End of London at a National Front/Anti-Nazi League demo, and this was where we were to be found for the next four Sundays. As usual, no casualties, but we had a couple of funny incidents. One was a local who walked up to a mounted police officer and asked if he could collect the horse manure as it was good for his roses. He was told it was all right and he took a plastic bag out of his pocket and proceeded to pick up the manure with his bare hands -- yuk! Another time I was walking by some horses with a tray of drinks when one of them decided that my pips on my shoulders looked like sugar lumps and so took a bite at them. This was just after he had eaten some oats, what a mess, oats and saliva all over my uniform and a bruised shoulder as well!

We were quite glad when these demos ended and to get back to our other regular events. Notting Hill had settled down with only trouble occurring late on Monday evening; still we will all remember being fed at Perk's Field this year. When we sat down under the large tent with our lunch of chicken, peas and boiled potatoes, someone noticed that it looked like we had sprinkling of parsley on our plate.

On careful inspection we realised that the parsley was baby spiders that had hatched in the roof of the tent in the heat and were now floating down onto us. The first "bush tucker trial". Then, for pudding we were given frozen yoghurts and plastic spoons, and I think every spoon snapped.

September saw us again taking part in a film, this time with Max Bygraves in a BBC TV appeal for funds for St John Ambulance; this was shown on the 1st of October at six thirty in the evening.

For ages, the members crewing the safety boat were looking for a course suitable to give them an official qualification and after many enquiries, booked a RYA power boat course with the National Sailing Centre at Cowes on the Isle of Wight. The bad news was that it would be on the 2nd and 3rd of December. So on the Friday

evening we all went by ferry to the centre. Good old Frank -- guess who felt sick just crossing the Solent?

The course was very thorough with us training on RIBs and a luggar (a type of boat with a diesel engine mounted in the middle and steered with a tiller) on the river Medina which was part river and part sea. At night-time we all, apart from Tina Parker, were sleeping in bunk beds in a dormitory. Unfortunately, one of us, Ron Bailey, snored, and he snored for England! First one then another of us went and found somewhere else to sleep. Ron came down next morning to breakfast wondering where everyone had gone, and when we told him why he denied that he ever snored. Just to add to the weekend it snowed on Sunday morning, which made our day on the water very interesting, and of course it would not be us without someone falling in the water, and guess who? Ron Bailey of course, who did the best walking on water I've ever seen. We all passed and returned home tired but feeling that we had achieved a lot that weekend.

A change in the structure of the Division during 1978 saw Les Blake taking over the running the Cadet Division as Superintendent and my wife Kate became his Divisional Officer.

Boxing Day sadly saw the last motorbike scramble at Pirbright. This was due to the Army saying that the bikes were eroding the common. That seemed odd. What about their tanks and four-wheel drives that used the land? My mother had a saying "As one door shuts another one will open" and as it turned out she was right. We now received lots of demand for the safety boat.

1979 started with us attending for the first time, a sailing event at the Queen Mary Sailing club called the "Bloody Mary." This is held in early January to coincide with the Boat Show at Earl's Court and could attract up to five hundred competitors. On the day the temperature was − 1, but the wind was kind to the sailors; just a nice breeze to fill their sails. The club is at the Queen Mary Reservoir at Ashford, Middlesex, and is one of the largest in southern England with an area of three square miles and a depth of forty feet.

A National Ambulance strike at the end of January had us taking the unit up to Waterloo on stand-by for two days before returning home early on a Wednesday morning in the snow.

In March, our boat, along with the four London District boats covered the Head of the River race. This is held on the Thames in the opposite direction to the Oxford and Cambridge boat race and on this occasion attracted four-hundred rowing eights. The St. John boats were stationed along the course with Thames Rescue boats which unfortunately did not carry radios. Due to the conditions of the wind against tide, the water became very choppy, especially around Hammersmith Bridge, which was our station, so extra boats were sent to join us. In fact though, it was the stretch between Fulham Football ground and Putney Bridge that had the major problems. The wind suddenly increased and within ten minutes there were eighteen rowing eights swamped, resulting in a hundred and sixty two rowers in the water. All of a sudden we received a radio message to get ourselves to Putney Reach urgently, and we spent the next twenty minutes pulling out rowers and taking them to the shore.

April saw us at Southall with the unit and ambulance for yet another National Front march and then the next weekend one in the East End, followed by one at the Pakistan Embassy, but all these passed off without too much trouble. Another change of venue for a pop concert for us was Wembley Stadium, where The Who played to near capacity audience; we treated twenty six casualties with one suffering a fractured jaw.

At the end of July, Kate and I took eight of the cadets to the National Camp at Bexhill for the first of many times, but I will be writing more about that later. Notting Hill this year turned out to be a sad affair, with a general broadcast informing us that Lord Mountbatten had been killed by a bomb in Northern Ireland. We attended his funeral later on, stationed by Westminster Abbey but as usual, just as I saw his horse walking at the front on the cortège with Lord Mountbatten's riding boots in the stirrups facing backwards, we were called to a casualty having a severe seizure and I missed all the rest; nothing changes.

Our ambulance was now eight years old and needed replacing. As a new one was out of the question due to the price, we sourced a replacement in a second-hand Bedford CF automatic from the London Ambulance  Service for £500. In November, we took delivery and then went about raising the funds. Our local, "The Queens Head," organised two charity walks for us and that was that; it was paid for. The end of the year came and instead of the Boxing Day Scramble we now had the Boxing Day sailing event at Queen Mary's.

****

Back in 1974, Nursing Officer Jean Nissen had joined the Division. Jean owned a local nursing home and quickly settled in with us, attending the duties that required us to take a nurse with us as well as other duties. It was much better that we took our own nurse than being given one from London District, some of who were very good but now and then we could end up with one who was a right pain in the neck. In 1975 Jean asked if her young son, Alexander Derek, (he preferred to be called Derek) could join. Although he was only just seventeen and not a cadet, she was desperate to get him some authority as he was starting to go off the rails and was lacking a male influence (his father had died when he was very young.) I became, over a period of time, like a big brother to him. He was young and could not keep his mouth shut, and this got him into trouble quite a few times, but over the years he became a very active member of the Division and grew up a bit, though he still had his moments.

In 1978 he got busted for being found with cannabis in his car, although he denied it was his and blamed one of his mates who was in the car when it was stopped and searched, but he still received a fine and a record; but that was Derek -- always in trouble but nothing too serious.

After that he seemed to mature, and by 1986 was promoted to Transport Officer. He and I had some wonderful times together when on duty; he was an excellent driver and knew London like the back of this hand. Once while on duty at Hyde Park we were sent by LAS control to a reported collapse, not breathing at Piccadilly underground station, so off we went on blues and twos up Oxford Street when we got stuck in a traffic jam. The next thing I knew was that we were travelling in the bus lane. I pointed out to Derek that we were going the wrong way when around the bend towards us came a double-decker bus. I just shut my eyes and the next thing I felt was a bump as we went up the kerb and statue of Eros flashed by my door. I asked Derek what happened to the bus and he just told me like it was an everyday occurrence -- "It just went up the one way street the wrong way and let us through."

We arrived at the station to find a girl resuscitating her punk dressed boyfriend who was vomiting blood, so we let her carry on until we got set up with our equipment. Just then, an LAS ambulance turned up and they took him in. We learned later that he did not survive and ironically two months later I saw the same man being interview on a recorded TV programme talking about solvent abuse in the underground, and how he did not do anything like that himself.

Again, while crewing together, this time at Trafalgar Square one New Years Eve, we were sent to an assault at an underground station. I cannot remember which one it was but it had the longest escalator of any one. Arriving, we found an LAS member already there and he started to make nasty comments about us and St John while we were dealing with the casualty. Derek whispered to me that there was something not right about this guy. Firstly, he had no badges on his uniform, and he didn't seem to know the right protocols. Derek then asked the guy which ambulance station he was from and he seemed a bit vague. Derek told me to hang on – "I'm going to get an LAS officer out to us." It turned out that this person was an LAS trainee from Waterloo and had been listening to our radio and trying to get to the incidents before the ambulances. He was fired from the LAS the following day. The officer stayed with us and showed us how to get our casualty who was on a carrying chair onto a moving escalator.

Derek had tried to join the LAS but due to his drug record was not accepted. He then became a first aid trainer for St John in London working with me, and we had many a laugh while working together. But after five years, as usual, his dodgy dealings and his mouth got him in trouble again and he left to start up his own business as a driving instructor.

At Notting Hill one year we had a guest with us, Dr Tony Blowers, Surrey's Commander, and he asked if he could go out on a shout [an incident that has been notified to you over the radio]. Derek and I took him, and as we were making our way through the crowd, he told him to close the sliding door and just as Tony asked him why, a big black arm grabbed him, at which point Derek just whacked the guy and said "That's why".

One duty that he was not allowed to do was at Buckingham Palace, due to the fact he had that conviction against him; still he had the last laugh when he attained his DOE Gold Award and went to the Palace to receive it from the Duke of Edinburgh. Derek became know as Del Boy after the character in "Only Fools and Horses" as he was still always up to some dodgy deal. Derek finally left the Division in 1989; his mother had left a few years earlier due to taking on a new larger nursing home, and after retiring from work was some years later, tragically crushed to death by a lorry in Walton High Street while standing on the pavement.

1980 began with a bit of a shock. We received a letter from Surrey County Council, the owners of our headquarters, saying that they wanted to sell the land, but as we were already sitting tenants we could purchase it for £12,500 or move and find other premises. Now, the idea of us being able to afford anywhere else in Weybridge was a non-starter, and £12,500 was a very good price, so the decision was made form an Appeals Committee to raise the money. We had in fact outgrown the HQ and were very short of space. The cadets had even moved back to Airscrew for meeting evenings due to the numbers attending. There was also a bit of a problem on a frosty night. When you left the HQ training room you could make the trip down the stairs in three painful bumps due to the frost on the steps. All the usual duties were being covered, and then in May we were surprised to learn that Weybridge had been awarded The Metropolitan Police Trophy for outstanding service in covering London events. This was the first time it had been awarded outside of London District. I made a good bit of press with this, which sowed the seeds with the local paper to do a full page spread on the history of the local St John and mainly on Weybridge and my family, as by now both my children had joined.

A couple of unusual boating duties happened in the summer. One was the Queen Mother's 80th birthday and one of the events was a tribute to her on the Thames ending with a firework display by the Houses of Parliament at ten thirty at night. Now, being on the River Thames is quite dangerous, even during daylight hours, but at least you can see anything large that's floating in the water. You can see any large wave caused by passing tugs and cruisers. You also have the tide to contend with and that can run at quite a fast speed. Now add into the equation the darkness of night time, plus all the reflections on the water of the lights on shore, and us with just a single light mounted on our boat, you can see the possibilities of an accident.

During the afternoon, we suddenly had trouble with the engine not giving us any power. The fault was found quite quickly; a headboard of a bed had jammed up between the stern and the engine. This was dealt with easily and the rest of the afternoon went by without incident. About nine thirty p.m., we were sent down to the other side of Tower Bridge. In those days our insurance covered us just past there; now we are non-tidal. It was getting dark, and as we passed under the bridge, all of a sudden, we felt the boat rising, and the next minute the engine started to scream. Then we crashed down with one hell of a bang. What had happened was that the tide was running out and as it funnelled through the bridge it formed a mini waterfall and we had taken off as we went over it. As they say, things happen in threes, and about an hour later, back on station, out from under a bridge came a Port of London boat bearing down on us and because we are so low in the water it had not seen us; a quick bit of manoeuvring at the last minute just saved us.

From the sublime to the ridiculous, the next boating duty was a twenty-four hour sailing event on the Welsh Harp in West London. This water was a large lake and in places was only six foot deep, and as sailing boats do not make any noise, after the experience on the Thames we had powerful spot lamps with us. That night there was hardly any wind and everything just glided on the water like ghost ships. As it was summer, gasses were being released from the bottom of the lake, so every now and then you would hear some really funny sounds and the smells! Well at first we started to blame each other on the boat before we found what was causing it.

Due to the pressure of work and his workplace being in the City of London, Cadet Superintendent Les Blake had to stand down from running the Cadets, leaving my wife in charge, so July saw us both taking thirteen Cadets with five adults (any excuse) to Bexhill camp for a week. (For a full account of Bexhill Camp, see Appendix 1). Then it was back to all the regular duties of demos, rugby etc; though in November we did attend the Cenotaph Remembrance Parade in Whitehall for the first time. It was very eerie. As the two minute silence started, the wind picked up and leaves were blown down past the Cenotaph as though they were the souls of the dead soldiers. The year finished as usual with a sailing event on Boxing Day, and us on duty at Trafalgar Square. Also in 1980, my daughter Sam was enrolled in the cadet Division.

1981 started with a bang, or rather with a blow, our first duty for the year being the annual Bloody Mary's race at the sailing club. This was wrecked by gale force winds and torrential rain that occurred half an hour after the start of the race. I have never seen conditions like it. We had waves that were four to five feet high. You could not see more then six feet around you. We had boats with masts torn off, sails ripped to shreds, some boat hulls split apart, others were sinking and many capsized. At one stage both my crewman (Derek) and I ducked as a small lightweight boat flew over the top of us before disappearing into the rain squall. We set about looking and found the poor sailor who had been thrown out. Out of the 262 boats that started the race, only 55 finished. The good news was no one was injured, and every one said that it was the worst conditions they had ever sailed in.

In February, the Division was awarded "Team of the Week" award on the BBC Radio 2 David Hamilton show, after someone locally had put us forward for this for all the good work we had done the month before. March was unusually busy with me on duty one Saturday at the local rugby club in the morning, followed by going to Twickenham in the afternoon, and then straight onto an exercise at Newlands Corner in the evening. It was a simulated air crash and meant us crashing around in snow in the woods searching for the casualties, and after being on duty all day we were really not in the mood for this. Then to cap it all, we were given a radio operator with an attitude problem from Raynet. His radio was a massive backpack and his call sign was so long it took ages to send anything. Finally, he fell down a ditch and had to be pulled out of the exercise, and no, we didn't push him!

The following week we received a request -- "Could we supply an ambulance and crew to cover the filming of car crashes at Brooklands from seven to seven for two days?" It sounded good, so some of us, including me, volunteered. Then came the bad news. It was from seven at night to seven in the morning. It transpired that they were making the film "An American Werewolf in London," and having done some filming in London they now needed to film cars, vans, taxis, and even a double-decker bus crashing into each other around a mock up of

Piccadilly Circus. Just to add more interest, when they were filming in London, it had rained, so they had to spray water all over the set. This was on a very cold March night and so led to it being very icy. They even ran out of cars to crash and at one time asked us if they could use the ambulance. We declined, though we would have been tempted if they'd have paid for a new one. It was very interesting to see how they made films and how the scenery was made; it not until you went round the back of it you saw all the bits of wood holding the facade up. At one point in the film the "police" charged into the "cinema" and the whole thing fell over backwards. While they were repairing it some of the actors came over and were talking to us, then one of them suddenly said "Are you guys for real?" They thought we were actors like them. Then the call went out -- "Could all of you please return the porno magazines to the shop which is next to the cinema." No, we did not have any. As for feeding arrangements, well you could have anything from a full English breakfast to duck a l'orange; all this at two a.m. on a cold March morning. It certainly put the police catering to shame.

Then finally at the end of March came the big one, after of course the Head of the River on the Saturday before, the first London Marathon. We were at the finishing line, which was at Constitution Hill just by Buckingham Palace. On the green next to the unit were two large recovery tents, equipped with one hundred and fifty mattresses laid on beds of straw. The weather was awful with a steady downpour of rain up to about two in the

afternoon. By this time, the floor inside the tents was just mud. The runners came in suffering from exhaustion, cramps and mild hypothermia and we treated sixty six runners on the Unit.

Then there was a twenty-four hour "lightning" strike by the London Ambulance Service and we were asked to supply an ambulance to cover the lower end of the M1 and A10 as these were thought to be high risk areas for accidents. In the end Steve and I only dealt with six calls all night.

One made us laugh afterwards. We were called to a restaurant where a man was unwell with possible heart problems. He was with a young lady who was his "escort" for the night. To be fair she accompanied him to the hospital, though the woman police officer with us said it was probably because he had not paid her.

The next large event was the Royal Wedding of Prince Charles and Lady Diana at the end of July. The Royal Wedding clashed with my week away with Kate at Bexhill camp, but everyone there said they would look after our cadets so Kate and I returned the night before and went on duty at the wedding before returning the following day the camp. The Division had been on duty the evening before the wedding at a massive firework display in Hyde Park where a quarter of a million people were watching the show, and had been kept busy treating a hundred and forty nine casualties, so it was good that we had some rested members on at the day of the wedding. The weather was beautiful and we were stationed on The Mall and someone (Del boy) had the bright idea to bring a portable TV with them so that we could watch what was going on at St Paul's. Suddenly while watching the TV we realised that a large crowd had gathered to watch as well. Although the numbers we treated were relatively small, only twenty six, we did have two with broken legs and one with a suspected spinal injury; all three had fallen out of trees while trying to see the procession. Ironically 16 years later I would be on duty at Princess Diana's funeral.

In September we changed the ambulance for another second-hand one from the LAS and also purchased another safety boat and trailer with a grant from the Queens Silver Jubilee Trust fund, so now we had two boats in the Division.

November was a bad month for us as when I arrived to go out on a local duty I found the back door of the HQ had been broken open and most of the equipment from inside the ambulance stolen, including stretchers, oxygen and splints etc; together worth over £2,000. Then we found out that the insurance did not cover us for all of the losses due to County misunderstanding the policy; still they did replace it all.

November saw my second visit to Buckingham Palace in a year. Earlier, I had taken the unit with crew to a garden party and arriving was directed by a police officer to the back of the palace. Once there, they then wanted it turned around but I was not allowed to turn on a wide bit of gravel, so had to do a umpteen point turn and while executing this, knocked over one of the Queen's standard rose bushes. The police officer just stuck it back in the ground saying "Don't worry, they won't notice it." This time we were at a DOE Award ceremony, and we were taken inside the palace down to the kitchen and given some food. On the way back I bumped into HRH the Duke of Edinburgh, who was lost and asked me how to get to the back garden. I was amazed how short he was but then the Queen is small and this gives you the impression that he is 6ft plus.

As Public Duty Officer, I was looking forward to a nice quiet time for December, and then I had a call. The weekend rugby was cancelled due to three inches of snow on the pitch. This was followed by another phone call from Steve to say we'd had a request to take a terminally ill patient home to, of all places Sunderland, where she wanted to die. Well I got it all organised. Del boy, Jean, his mum to nurse the patient, and Tina Parker who filled in at the last minute when some else dropped out were all signed up for it. We tried to postpone the trip for a few days for better weather but were told the patient might not live that long, so after checking the weather report and travel, it seemed that we could do the three-hundred mile round trip, as no more snow was forecast in the north east of England, though it was forecast for the west country.

Well they left at nine a.m. after we dug the twelve inches of snow away from the garage doors. I received a phone call at three thirty. They had arrived. There was hardly any snow after Luton and they were returning straightaway. Now the problems started. The snow that had been forecast for the southwest had in fact turned up in the Midlands and North East and at five thirty I received a reverse charge phone call from Blyth in Nottingham. It was Del boy. They had run into a snow drift and broken down; a passing police car had come to their aid and had pulled them out and taken them to a nearby hotel and they would try again tomorrow. Next morning, another phone call, the alternator had seized and the local garage was working on it. They finally left Blyth at one thirty and because it was still snowing would use the M1 but half an hour later I got another phone call. They were in a service station with a misfire, and eventually they returned to Weybridge at six o'clock that evening.

A fortnight later we received a letter from the relatives thanking the crew for taking their mum home in such horrible weather and letting us know that she had died a week later in her own home as she had wanted.

The final duty of the year was of course New Years Eve at Trafalgar Square, but this time due to the size of the crowds it turned into a bloody New Years Eve with us treating 115 casualties and taking nine to hospital in our ambulance.

****

After last year with the gales at the Bloody Mary, 1982 brought snow and ice to contend with at the same event. It had been snowing a couple of days before and true to form we had driving snow and mist to put up with; we were beginning to think it was us causing the bad weather each year. But apart from being covered in snow and ice, and wishing we were somewhere warm, the sailing event went off with hardly anything for us to do.

In May the second London Marathon took place. After last years very wet and soggy finish in the park, the finish had been moved to Westminster Bridge and County Hall was the main treatment area with rooms inside to treat casualties and us outside to treat any overflows. I asked and got permission to video us, and to bring Sam, my daughter, as it was her birthday that day (14th).

The film was from us leaving our HQ to covering the event and back to base as a record of what was involved, and was intended to be shown to the public, or if needed for fundraising. We left at eight o'clock in the morning and returned after treating a hundred and eighty runners at six o'clock. The video, after editing went from four hours to just twenty minutes, and it was brilliant. It had been taken by a friend of Del boy's and not a member of St John. It showed St John at its best -- working in the unit and out on the pavement, dealing with everything from collapses, to cramp and huge blisters. The runners at the end were given a medal, a foil blanket, a bottle of water and a Mars bar, and if they ate the Mars bar then drank the cold water, the result was it all came back up. Nice one!

I had for some time been on the side of the women in the Division, on account of the fact that the grey dresses they had to wear were totally impractical for outdoor duties. Though they had both an indoor and outdoor uniform listed, when we attended both the London Marathon and the Derby in June, the Duty Orders stated that grey dresses were to be worn. On the London duty, they did as they were ordered, but for the Derby they wore the outdoor uniform of black jumpers and trousers with white shirts. This caused uproar from certain County staff. "They must wear dresses when the Queen is around," I was told. My reply was, firstly, we are not likely to treat, let alone be seen by her. Secondly, as we were stationed by the gipsy village, I was not prepared to have our women in dresses that gaped when they bent over, and when treating, people could look up their skirts. It got so heated that I ended up saying that if they were worried about it, then Weybridge would not come to the Derby next year. Shortly after this I received a request from London District, asking if I would come and show the video of the London Marathon at a weekend conference later in the year. The audience would be made up of doctors, nurses and surgeons from across England. Well you could not say no could you, so later in the year up I went to London District's HQ, feeling a bit intimidated, especially after being told I was following a talk by a Army Medical Major from the 3rd Paras on the action of medics treating injured soldiers in the Falklands War. Watching and listening to his talk, it dawned on me that though the trauma injuries were on a larger scale then what we dealt with; gunshots and blast injuries as well as the burns that occurred on Sir Galahad when bombed in Bluff Cove, it was still basic first aid although on a grander scale, i.e. water on burns and if it's bleeding, stop it.

After a short break, it was my turn. Thank goodness for the Marathon video. Our station was under a loudspeaker and that plus the rustling of the foil blankets, all picked up by the recording, caught the atmosphere on the day. At the end there were a lot of questions about both the duty and our mobile unit, and then finally one from Cathy Stratton, a London District Nursing Officer. She asked why the women were wearing dresses, after she had seen them squatting on the pavement treating runners who were sitting on chairs. I answered saying, "Well that's what your Orders state they must wear." "Ridiculous!" she said. Afterwards at lunch, we were talking and she said she had no idea that members on mobile units were put in that position and she would see about sorting it out. Also, the Major spoke to me saying how impressed he was, and he would not like to have to treat that many civilians. All in all it was a good day, especially when Orders came out later that year for New Years Eve and the Marathon that outdoor uniform was to be worn, and lo and behold, the Derby was the same. This probably started the demise of the hated grey dresses.

Two contrasting events took place at Wembley Stadium, one in late May, when Pope John Paul II held a mass there. Interestingly, it was reported that someone had come up with the info that with the numbers, and the age of the audience there could be nine deaths, so nine coffins were under the stage! In fact, it was a very quiet duty and no one died. Three weeks later we were back, this time for The Rolling Stones World Tour concert; how about that for extremes?

Notting Hill this year was quiet compared to previous years, We had a medical student attached to us. Now sometimes these students were a right pain with the attitude of "I'm in charge, and I don't need to clear up after me," -- that was a nurse's job. So when we were told that a student doctor was to be put on our station we groaned; how wrong we were.

David Penman walked up and after introducing himself, asked what we wanted him to do. "I don't mind if it's making the tea, or major surgery." He became a great friend of ours and would always ask to be put on our unit

if it was out on duty. David disappeared for a couple of years, and unbeknown to us had gone to work abroad in Fiji. When he came back in 1985 he contacted us and came out on duty again; the most memorable being the Derby that year, when he changed into his Fijian St John uniform. This was a wrap over shirt and white top. He even did an interview on TV on the unit while wearing it; some of the County HQ staff were not too amused about it though.

In November I experienced the most moving duty so far, when Weybridge were invited to attend the Festival of Remembrance at the Royal Albert Hall. The ceremony was itself moving, but when the two minute silence took place and the poppy petals fell from the ceiling, it was indescribable. Then of course to be on duty at the Cenotaph the following morning was the final touch.

Also in November my son Neil was enrolled as a Cadet; now all the family were in St John, though he did not stay in for long. All through the year the Division and the Appeals Committee had been busy fundraising and slowly the funds were mounting. They raffled a second-hand car; the winning ticket being drawn by Joe Glormly at a race meeting at Kempton Park, and held a sponsored sailing race at Queen Mary's -- just two of many events that took place.

The year ended with a terrible tragedy at Trafalgar Square on New Years Eve. Having covered this event since 1972 and subject to any adverse weather conditions, we had seen a steady increase to the numbers of cases treated each year. Our unit was always stationed at King Charles Island, just south of Nelson's Column along with another from London District. This year the weather was mild and the Square was packed with an estimated thirty thousand revellers, with another thirty five thousand people around it.

Just after midnight as usual we started to get casualties being brought in. Most of these were caused by glass, as this year for some unknown reason, people were throwing their empty wine bottles and beer cans up in the air and into the crowd. The resulting broken glass on the ground and in the fountains caused some terrible cuts to feet as well as serious head injuries. At about twelve thirty a.m., we were requested to send our doctor to the south east corner junction with the Strand, just fifty yards away; a barrier had collapsed and some people were seriously hurt. It turned out that two women had been trampled to death; one came from Woking.

That night seventy-nine revellers were treated on our unit, with minor cuts being stitched onboard, and ten more casualties were removed to hospital. Looking at the pictures I took at this time of us working, the one thing that stuck me in those days, was that no-one wore gloves, not even the doctors when stitching; how times have changed. The seven of us finally returned to our HQ at four thirty in the morning after having left at seven thirty the night before.

****

1983 started with an unusual "Bloody Mary" -- at long last a fine sunny day, with blue skies and although a bit chilly, just the right amount of wind to make a very pleasant day. We had all the other usual duties, and Steve, Bob and I were involved with fundraising for the new HQ, but more about that later. We had also followed the Cadets in having to find somewhere else to train, due to the lack of space at the HQ. First we tried our local, "The Queens Head," but this proved to be a disaster as most of us including me, spent most of the time in the bar. Next we changed meeting nights to Wednesday as it was the only evening available at the local ATC hall at Brooklands. This was even worse as the attendance dropped down to only three to five members turning up. It's funny, but you would have thought after often being out both Saturday and Sunday, the members would have liked a break from St John until the middle of the week, but it was not what they wanted. We then moved back to meeting on Monday evenings at the tennis pavilion at St George's College, and instantly we were back to the usual numbers.

We were back outside County Hall for the third London Marathon in May, but unfortunately it rained before the start, making a lot of runners wet and cold, and if you start like that it is going to be hard, as they found out. We had our own runner taking part, a Mr Paul Thomas, who had offered to run and raise money for our HQ appeal. He arrived at the finish, his time having been three and a half hours and he was not in a bad state, looking fit enough for me to get some photographs for our local papers, with the news that he had raised over £300. Some of the other runners were not so lucky, with exhaustion, mild hypothermia and severe cramps. One runner was wearing what I thought were red socks. In fact he had lost his running shoes  and socks the day before and had run in brand new ones; his socks were red from blood as he had run on blisters which had burst and bled. Another had no idea where he was and what he had been doing that day due to the hypothermia he was suffering from; how he finished the race I have no idea. Altogether, we treated over a hundred runners.

In June, Kate became Divisional Superintendent of the cadets, with Cathy Roots, an SRN becoming her Divisional Officer, while her husband Paul was a Divisional Officer with the adults.

The first Saturday of July was our Flag Day, but this was suddenly cut short when we were told that the HQ had to be emptied that week-end as the demolition of it was due to start on the following Monday. It was all hands to the pumps. I ended up with one of the safety boats in my front garden; the other one went to Del boy's friend's garage. The ambulance went and stayed with the mobile unit on the airfield at BAC, and all the other bits and bobs went all over the place, but by Sunday evening it was cleared. This was on top of duties that we'd attended that weekend.

The end of July saw a request for first aid cover at the Brooklands Society Reunion meeting. Someone had decided that they should have us there as the meeting was getting a large attendance; this was their fifteenth year. The aim of the society was to try and keep the track and the buildings of the old Brooklands racing circuit in good condition and raise money to have a museum there, as it was the first oval racing circuit ever built. A. V. Roe, later Avro, Hawkers and Vickers Aviation had been based there, the first Hawker Hurricane had flown from the airfield, and Wellington bombers were manufactured there during WWII. It had a very long history with both the racing car and the development of flying.

On this reunion day pre-war cars and motorbikes turned up in their hundreds, and so did the crowds; the weather was glorious. I went and asked if we could hold a blanket collection at the exit when the day had finished as we were fundraising ourselves for the HQ and to my surprise was told that would be okay, and they even gave us a plug over the tannoy. We stationed four of us at the exit, two on either side of the road, and collected over £250; this started a tradition that would last for some years.

In September, we sold our first safety boat as it was becoming impossible to run both. Mainly, it was the towing, and the number of crews needed to man it. The rest of the year settled down with all the usual duties and the year ended with New Years Eve at Trafalgar Square. After last year's trouble, the fountains were emptied and boarded up, the area around was free of traffic, and the revellers were searched and all bottles and tins were confiscated. We treated only eight casualties compared to the seventy nine the year before, but true to form we (Weybridge) still found some action. After being stood down at two a.m., while travelling home, as we came into Battersea Rise, what should we come across but a crashed car up a lamppost? We all piled out to find the driver but he was nowhere to be seen. The female passenger was still in the car with injuries; the odd thing she was topless. We never did find out why, we could only guess.

When the Fire Brigade arrived I heard a fireman speaking to his control and when asked if he needed any medical assistance replied "You should see what we have got here, a St John ambulance, a doctor and the biggest ambulance I've ever seen (our mobile). I think we are all right for the next war."

****

In February 1984, MD 901, our safety boat suffered catastrophic damage when after a non-eventful "Bloody Mary." In January, the club had allowed us to leave it moored on the water rather the having to take it back to my house. I thought it would be safer there then in my front garden. My worry was always it could be vandalised or stolen. Unfortunately one night a strong gale blew up and all night it raged before blowing itself out by the morning. I received a phone call at nine o'clock telling me I had better come up to the club because our boat was damaged. Luckily I only work round the corner. On arrival I found that the only one of nine boats that had broken its mooring was ours. The gale had blown it onto the concrete shore and it had been battered to bits. On first examination the engine was missing, then we found it still attached by the control cables hanging six feet under the boat in the water; well what was left of it. As for the boat itself, the transom, where the engine normally was fitted was smashed and the triple hull was now a single hull with three massive five foot holes. The engine was a write-off, and soon replaced.

The boat would only take a fortnight to repair but before they could start, it had to be drained of water first and that would take over two months of it standing up on end draining out. The interesting bit was filling out the insurance claim, especially when saying who you held responsible for the accident. Ironically it would not be the only time I would be blaming the weather for damaging our vehicles.

On a brighter note, Sam my daughter, much to my pride gained her Grand Prior badge; the first at Weybridge since Frank Staff gained his in 1954, and of course I got full news coverage with that story. While all this was going on, we were still fundraising and the HQ was beginning to take shape.

Our station was in a different place for the London Marathon this year, at the Isle of dogs, which is about the halfway point. It is called "the wall" by the runners. This time, we were now into repairing the runners; it was massaging runners' calf muscles and thighs, and padding blisters so that they could continue the race. In all we treated a hundred and seventy nine of them.

In June, we received a pamphlet from Windsor Safari Park for a special reduced day rate for St John Ambulance, and as the cadets had their summer camp, we decided to take the juniors out for the day. Sadly the Safari Park has now gone; it's been replaced by Legoland, and the Badgers now have a special day once a year. The Park was great for the youngsters, with a lion enclosure, a water display with dolphins and two killer whales and all the trappings of a zoo. Our lot loved it, though I left Kate to explain to them about the rhinos, as while we were sitting down having our packed lunch near the enclosure they noticed two rhinos getting amorous, until the female sprayed the male in his face with her pee; it was like a fire hose going off. The other bit of news that happened in July was that I was made a Serving Brother of the Order, *[the historic order of St John, headed by HM the Queen and with its own system of honours just for St John members]* which was a nice surprise.

For the first time since we took the duty, it rained at Notting Hill, and on both days. Although we were stationed on a junction by Ladbroke Grove, and saw a lot of carnival, it was unbelievably quiet, but as usual being Weybridge, after being stood down early on the Monday and then diverted out of the area by a different route, what did we come across? A road accident. One car had driven full speed into a stationary car at a crossing. The result was one fatality, and four others seriously injured along with some bystanders suffering shock from witnessing the accident. The lasting memories I have of this incident were yellow tennis balls, and I mean loads of tennis balls -- (one of the cars had a boot full of them, and they were spilled all over the road), and also our female doctor, who was treating one of the seriously injured when an LAS crew turned up. One of them looked like he had just got out of bed. He was unshaven, had no tie and his shirt was opened to the middle of his chest. His opening remark of "OK love, stand back and let the professionals take over," was probably not the best. She turned on him and asked "Who the hell are you? Where's your tie and do up your shirt, and I'm not your love, I'm a Doctor!" He ran back to the Ambulance and reappeared shortly with his shirt buttoned up and wearing his tie.

After taking on the job of press officer for the Division back in 1972, I don't know whether it was luck or what but I always seemed to be in the right place at the right time for stories that interested the press, and of course one tended to build a good relationship with the local papers and a good reputation as well with them. So in November when not one but three seventeen year old new members joined, and being triplets, it was too good a story not to use and the local papers snapped it up.

It was back to film work in December. I received a call from another Division, they had been covering some film work at Worplesdon Common over the weekend but it had overrun and they could not cover the extra day, so could we help. Del boy and I were available so after checking it was day time filming, after the last time, we duly turned up at 9:00 a.m. The location was in a pub car park; with again, film catering; lovely full English breakfast to start the day off. The film starred Meryl Streep in a World War II film and we were there because they were filming a parachutist supposedly landing in France at night. They had already been in France but had fallen out with the authorities, and had been refused permission to do any flying there, so the film company had found a site locally to do the landing.

On day one it was too sunny, so at four o'clock we went home. On day two, there was thick fog that did not clear all day, and on day three it snowed. Finally on day four they decided it was do or die. The idea was a parachutist would leap out of a helicopter, landing at a designated place were the cameras would film him. While talking to the guy he told us that because they wanted him to use an original 1940's style chute he could not steer the thing and with the downdraft of the helicopter he had no idea were he might end up. He was right. On the first attempt he ended up in a tree, the second saw him disappear into the next clearing, and finally on the third attempt, he made it. Interestingly I was asked what the daily charge was to cover the filming and I quoted £100 a day. They then queried why the other Division only charged £50 a day so I said that was their problem, and asked if we were too expensive? Turned out the film company thought that the other Division was very cheap, and wondered if they had made a mistake.

1984 ended with the usual duties but at least the HQ was built and had a roof on it though no doors or windows as we had run out of money again. Due to problems at the Airscrew Social club when it got doubled-booked with a darts tournament twice and other events, the cadets had now moved to the old Red Cross hall in Weybridge.

Well third time lucky -- after two unsuccessful attempts at resus to date, where the casualties had not survived, one of my work colleagues had an accident at work and I was called to the workshop where he was lying, eyes open and dilated, mouth open, and not breathing. Checking that someone had sent for an ambulance, I commenced resus. It's bad enough resuscitating a workmate, but when his nick-name was Concorde due to his long nose -- did I have trouble in sealing his nose, and it got in the way of the mouth to mouth! Anyhow I gave two breaths followed by checking the pulse—no sign -- fifteen compressions followed by two breaths again, another fifteen compressions and as I went to give the next two breaths, I noticed he blinked, and as I went to put my mouth over his he said "I'd rather you didn't do it" or words to that effect. Basically F*** OFF. I jumped back thinking oops I've got carried away in resuscitating him. He was taken to hospital and for some time afterwards, I was known as the parts manager that kisses mechanics. Mind you, every time we met up for a drink, most Fridays after work, he would buy me a drink with the comment "I owe you my life" -- quite embarrassing. One day we were talking and he suddenly informed me that when the accident happened, all he could remember was floating towards a bright light and feeling totally at rest and peaceful, when all of a sudden he could hear me swearing at him from behind and then he was pulled back from the light and opened his eyes to see me trying to kiss him. I then remembered that my mates did tell me I was swearing at him while I was working on him.

Years later I met his wife while teaching a first aid course and her opening comment was "Hello Ray. Do you know that you're the sod that stopped me collecting my husband's insurance?" then burst out laughing.

With the letter from Surrey County Council (S.C.C.) at the beginning of 1980 saying in simple terms buy or lose it; the HQ that is. The Division set about looking how we could raise the asking price of £12,500. At one of these meetings, I think it was Bob Hutton, put forward the idea that we might see if we could also purchase an extra piece of land from the S.C.C. to square up the property. They owned the next building to us Stretton Lodge and used it as a drugs counselling clinic. After some long and protracted negotiations which took up most of the year it was agreed to, raising the total to £16,000. It was also decided that to have a chance of getting donations from companies we would have to have someone with a few letters after their name to give some credence. I know that we advertised. I cannot remember how it came about, but a gentleman, a Lt. Col. Adrian Tansley, retired, came forward and with my wife as his secretary started writing to local and not so local companies for donations; this resulted in donations from Sir Cliff Richard, Sir Robert Marks, former Metropolitan Police Commissioner and many others including £5 from the local Brownie pack. Charity walks were organised by our local, The Queens Head and Airscrew with a whopping £3,200 from four walkers who walked over the Pennines from the Weybridge and Byfleet Rotary Club. The target was achieved in eighteen months which surprised us and county staff. Even before we had reached this amount someone, either Bob or Steve Smith had floated the idea that maybe we should carry on and raise enough money for a new HQ, estimated at £55,000

In those days, there were no grants from the County of St John in Surrey -- not like today where loans and part payment for ambulances are excepted things and new HQs are built for the Divisions. There was no help; you had to fund it yourself. A new Appeal Committee was formed as this was going to be a much bigger venture. It was made up of our President, Mr Alan Baker, the owner of Haslets, a haberdashery shop on the corner of Church Road in Weybridge (now an opticians, though the corner is still called Haslet's corner), Vice President, Mr Harry Cohen, an Elmbridge councillor, Bob, Steve and myself. Through Harry, a Mr Mark Warner, who owned a printing business at Addlestone and finally Mr Tony Pidgley, the Managing Director of Berkeley Homes, a local high-class building company, who happened to be looking to do something for the local community, and as a builder was just what we required.

Tony was an amazing and colourful character; a self-made man who originated from a well-known family of travellers but now built expensive houses in the area. His grasp of the Anglo-Saxon, i.e. swearing was interesting, and if he wanted something done, it was done now, not next week or month. He was the one who said that just to try and raise the money and leave it in a bank before starting any building was not an option, as we would be like a dog chasing its tail; as fast as we made money the cost would have gone up and we would never achieve it.

He urged that what we should do was to knock down the existing HQ, then we could publicise our situation, raise some money, use it to build what we could, stop, and then do the publicity all over again. This showed people what we had achieved so far and that we meant to carry on until it was finished. To be honest he was right and of course you did not argue with him. Having agreed this strategy, the Committee then proposed a corporate boxing night to be the main fundraiser for next year. Tony's right-hand man and Commercial Director of Berkeley Homes was Paul Read, and he was given the job of organising this event. So local fundraising continued in the meantime, including by a friend of mine, Mr Paul Thomas, who ran the London Marathon and raised £300. This might not seem much today, but in 1983 this was a lot of money. In July we received a phone call from Tony saying he wanted the HQ cleared out in three days, as his demolition crew was ready to start; they did and reduced it to rubble within a fortnight. We purposely left the large St John Ambulance, Weybridge sign up so anyone would know who owned the land, and we got the people who had to do community work, (minor offenders), to dig out the footings, and by the end of the year the foundations were laid.

The plans for the new HQ had been drawn up in 1982 and would include a meeting hall, and enough garage space for all our vehicles. The one problem was that we were restricted to a single storey building due to rules about buildings being near main roads and the River Wey. As one can see today, this regulation does not apply any more.

By the beginning of 1984, the Boxing night was up and running and was scheduled for March. Barclay Homes had organised the venue (Thorpe Park corporate centre), the boxing club would supply the boxers and the ring, and the referees. Mark Warner had printed all the advertising posters and the tickets; the only thing we had to supply was the first aid cover for the evening and a doctor. County were shocked to hear what we were up to, and even more shocked to learn that the cost for all this was about £3,000; in fact Steve had a letter from our Commissioner accusing him, and us, of being irresponsible in jeopardising that amount of funds. They still wanted to attend though and thought they would get in free; wrong.

Well, what a night. Four hundred attended at £15 per head -- a dinner jacket and black tie event, a very good meal, followed by a raffle, then boxing bouts; an auction, then more boxing. While this was going on there was a tote with betting as well, and at the end of the night we had raised over £16,000 profit towards the HQ. I could not resist looking over to the St John table and just smiling sweetly at them.

So within a few weeks, building material started to be delivered to the site, and each week more would appear. Builders then started to work. One day I asked one of them if he was there permanently. He said no; he and the others were just turning up in between other jobs in the area. By the end of July it had walls, a roof and windows, but no doors or any interior. Still it now was looking like our HQ and as usual we had run out of funds. At a meeting in September another Boxing night was then planned but these things take time to organise and being practical, the earliest it could be held would be next March. All through the winter we carried on fundraising but we really needed a big injection of money to complete it. Then Steve dropped a bombshell. He had found a replacement for the mobile unit -- a forty foot left-hand drive Across Trust Jumble Ambulance that he had seen advertised. Well I must admit that I thought, my God we have not finished the HQ and there he is spending more money that we have not got. Not only that, but the HQ had been designed for our existing unit which was thirty eight foot long and three RSJs were mounted at the back of the garage to stop us crashing out through the back.

Anyhow that's another story; just to say Barclay Homes donated the money needed for the new unit, and they cut out the RSJs so that it would fit in the garage with just six inches to spare. The second boxing night took place in March, but the profit was not as good as the year before. One of the reasons was that during the previous year a couple of boxers had died in a ring and another had been seriously injured and the negative publicity had put a lot of people off boxing. We also had a devil of a job to find a doctor prepared to even attend the event. Also that night, we had employed some young scantily dressed girls to go round the tables collecting money, but we noticed that some of them kept going to the toilets before handing in the money. At the end of the night the takings for the raffle did not add up, so you live and learn and not to do that again.

While this was going on one of the Committee had heard that Walton Charities had funds available for local projects in the Elmbridge area. He had approached them to see if we could get some help as we were still short of the final target; the difference was really between making do, to finishing it off in style.

At the same time something had been worrying me. Every time I visited the building, it seemed to me as if the roof for the ambulance garage was too low and more than once I spoke to Steve about this, but he dismissed it saying that they had the measurements and they knew what they were doing. Eventually I nagged so much that one day we got a ladder and guess what -- they had the size of the ambulance but it did not include the extra one foot height of the blue lights. The roof could not be raised as it was the main support of the main roof. So the next best thing they did was they lowered the floor by one foot; that's why there is a step from the hall into the garage and why the ambulance's garage floor is lower then the rest. That was the bad news, and then came the good news.

Walton Charities were so impressed with what we had achieved, they donated a large amount of money to finish off the project; not only that but when Steve was talking to them he made a casual remark that our ambulance would need replacing soon. Would you believe it, they turned round and said "Why did you not ask at the same time as you asked of the HQ. How much is a new one?" At this time a new ambulance was £18,000, and we were told to go ahead and order one -- what a result.

By the 1st June everything was finished -- we had flower beds, and a car park laid with gravel, (that turned out to be a pain as it all got walked into the HQ), but it was ready for an official opening next month, at which the past Commissioner Dr Hicks quietly spoke to Steve and apologised about the letter, and said that they (County) should have trusted Weybridge, and well done.

****

With Steve informing us that he had found a replacement for the mobile unit, the Jumbulance, (and to be fair our Mk II was over twenty years old), we now had to look into what was needed to convert it into a unit for our use. The unit itself was huge; not only forty foot long but twelve foot six inches high, and apart from being left hand drive, it also had a six speed gear box -- this was going to be fun I thought. Inside, it had a double rack of stretchers, eight in total with sixteen seats, a toilet and a full kitchen looking like an aircraft galley with a small fridge, cooker and four water containers. Access was via a hydraulic lift at the rear and a normal coach door at the front.

Just to give you a bit of background on the Across Trust and this unit, this charitable organisation was formed in September 1972 with the aim of transporting groups of terminally sick and handicapped to and from Lourdes in France. The journey took about twenty two hours with a six hour turn-round, loading with a group transported the previous week for the return trip. They now had a fleet of five Jumbulances.

This one was the first and was always referred to as "Old Mk 1, the love bus". It had started life, though with a different body on it, due to an accident when while empty, it had rolled down an embankment. A new Van Hool body had been fitted with a completely redesigned interior. She (we always referred to the unit as "she") had in the eleven years of her life, travelled over a one and a half million miles, and in 1983 had a new engine fitted. The reason they were selling her was one of the engine liners was scored, which meant that she used a large amount of oil when on a trip. They were also looking to replace her with a Mk. VI, a Jumbo Jumbulance; a bendy bus that would take double the pilgrims. The asking price had been £26,000 but we finally purchased it for £12,500 with the donation from Barclay Homes paying for it.

All it left for us was to design the interior and find someone to do the work. Well, we kept the design group relatively small as from experience if the group was too big we spent all the time arguing and not getting very far. Also, most of use had been involved in the other mobile unit, so between Steve, Bob, Frank Staff, Jean Nissen our Nursing Officer, Derek, Kate and myself we came up with a design after many meetings. We did contemplate keeping the double bank of stretchers but it was not practical, we had long debates about the toilet whether to keep it or not; the women won and it stayed. Now to find some one to do the conversion, having been turned down by the Apprentice School at British Aero Space, formally Vickers Aviation at Brooklands. But when they saw her they changed their mind as there was so much for them to do, from the re-wiring to take 240V lighting, the constructing of the surgery unit, and the cutting out and fitting of our stretchers. They designed and tested a set of steps that would fit under the side ramp with a handrail that could be folded when not in use and stowed underneath in one of the compartments; all we had to pay for was the materials. As luck would have it, she was mainly white with only a two foot wide stripe down the full length and across the front and back, and as my brother-in-law ran his own body repair and paint shop locally, guess who "volunteered?" It's nice to have contacts.

By the beginning of June she was finished. Our old Mk. II attended its last event, a London Rowing Club Regatta held at the lake at Thorpe Park. Ironically Mk. III's first duty was the Trooping of the Colour (as was Mk. I), so this time at least we could start her life with a nice quiet duty, followed by the Derby and then a Brooklands Reunion meeting, where yet again we did a blanket collection, raising over £286.

Then we had just one week to get everything ready for the official opening by the Lord Prior Sir Maurice Dorman on the 7th July. If it did not move, it got painted; well nearly. Then a panic the new ambulance would not be delivered in time for the opening. In fact, it was still in Ireland where it was still being made. After a lot of phone calls, a compromise was found. A new ambulance being delivered to another county would be diverted to us just for the weekend so we could have one for the opening ceremony. It was also decided that on the day we would have Mk. III not at the HQ, but parked round the corner and would then have it arrive at the end of the ceremony for dramatic affect.

Sunday was a lovely sunny day; it could not have been better. A large group of guests came and we had a full turnout of the membership. The Lord Prior informed us that it was his first visit to Surrey, and the first time ever that he had to open a new HQ and dedicate two new vehicles. Everything went well and then the mobile slowly drove up to the HQ -- what an entrance!

After everything had finished, Del boy took the unit for a short trip up St Peters Way in Chertsey. I then got a phone call; he had broken down and after failing to get it started, we had it towed to BAC as we would not be able to park it at the HQ. Back to basics -- check the fuel. It showed half a tank of fuel and as the tank holds a hundred gallons, it seemed alright. A friend of Del's was a commercial mechanic and came out on Monday evening to find out what was wrong. After a few checks he found that no fuel was getting to the engine and thinking that maybe the tank had some sludge in the bottom of it, he decided to drain the tank. So the following day, there we were with a lot of empty cans, and as luck would have it, she had a bump valve fitted, but when he opened it nothing came out -- bone dry.

When we rang Across Trust they told us "Sorry, we meant to tell you -- the gauge is faulty don't let it get below ½ full." Nice one! Twenty gallons of diesel later and after bleeding the system she was up and running.

July saw the last attendance at Runnymede Pleasure Park as the crowds were no longer going there and therefore we were not needed. We also had the first B.B.Q. at the HQ; this has now become a bit of a tradition, with any excuse used to hold one.

Notting Hill this year was back to the hot summer weather and crowds, and due to our size we were in yet another location, on the main route. We saw all the floats with the bands, and still we ended up treating eighty six casualties over the two days. Our HQ had been designed with an electric door for the ambulance bay and a manual door for the mobile. For the first few months all worked well with the electric one, though the clearance between the top and the blue lights was only two inches. But one day, I had a phone call from Ginny Johnson saying that as she had driven out, she had smashed both of the blue lights. I checked everything but could not find why it had happened until a week later when I went to take out the ambulance myself and noticed that as the door went up, it then jumped back a couple of inches. It would have taken off the replacement lights. We called out the engineers, who could not understand why it had happened but did a few adjustments and showed us how to manually work the door, but it meant getting up in the roof of the garage to do it. This seemed to cure the problem though. Then a month later, it happened again, and then again, and then the chain drive broke; this time with the door half way up, and there was a vehicle parked underneath the hatch to the loft -- we were seriously pissed off.

After a lot of discussions with the manufacturers of the doors, it transpired that the electric motor was not powerful enough to lift the door and what was needed was a three phase motor and three phase supply which was not available in our area. The door was converted to a manual lift.

The beginning of November started off well for me, being on duty at Brooklands Museum to witness the 50th anniversary of the first flight of the Hawker Hurricane from Brooklands in 1935 and seeing a Hurricane fly in and land on the runway at BAC. After that things went a bit downhill.

In November, Kate had an accident with her car and rather than it getting written off, I went to the local scrap yard to get a replacement door and whilst there I managed to drop it onto my foot, severely damaging my little toe. All the scrap yard had in a first aid kit was an eye dressing, so I used that and then drove myself to the A&E at St Peters. On arrival, what should be there but our ambulance – great, that means the members will get to know. Worse still, I was taken on a wheelchair by a porter; yes you can guess by one of the Divisional members. Then we bumped into Del Boy and his mum who were visiting a friend in hospital. At least our

Divisional doctor was not the one who put in the ten stitches that my toe needed. All this on my birthday; still it made a good story for the local papers.

Now with our own HQ we could have a Christmas party for both the cadets and us adults, before finishing the year with our usual boat duties on Boxing Day at QMSC followed by New Years Eve at Trafalgar Square.

****

1986 turned out to be a year that would see some major changes in my life. At the beginning of the year we received requests for our services at two major golf events at Wentworth. The first would be the PGA in May and the other in October; the World Match Play. We also had an enquiry from Ash Vale Division asking if we would be interested in covering on a rota, the stock car racing at Tongham, which was just outside Aldershot but within the Surrey boundaries and took place every Thursday evening starting at seven thirty p.m. and with the odd Saturday and a meeting on Boxing Day.

Having discussed this duty with Steve and then with the members, and looking at the logistics of getting to Tongham by seven we took it on. There was also one other Division on the rota -- Cranleigh, and with Ash

Vale, the rota became jokingly known as "CranAshBridge."

In April while at the Greater London Council Farewell Party (it was closing down), we were called to two casualties who had both been sprayed with a chemical of unknown source, and were now having breathing difficulties. I dispatched them to St Thomas' in our ambulance, which nearly shut down the A&E and put the crew of three in hospital overnight. The reason was that the chemical was CS gas and by being in the confined space of the ambulance and on the clothing of the casualties, it carried on contaminating everyone – Ooops!

In May, I received a phone call from National Headquarters. They had an author who was writing a book about St John and wanted to interview Kate and I on our experiences. This was done whilst on duty at a quiet demo, and we then brought him back to Weybridge to continue.

I found out at the beginning of June that having worked in the motor trade since leaving school, the company I worked for was going to close. Although I knew that it was coming, I would find myself out of a job by October. As Transport Officer I was not only looking after our fleet of vehicles but also the public duties, organising the duties and members as well as the PR work. Then Bob Hutton, who was now the Area Commissioner, rang up and asked if we could have a meeting at our HQ. I thought that it might be to talk about my knack of doing something first and telling County afterwards, or that I been found out on one of my many deals? But no, it was not that. Steve had resigned from St John and I asked if I would be interested in taking over the Division; if not, County would have to find someone. What a bombshell. I could not believe it. I had no idea this was about to happen. It seemed that Steve had had enough after all the work in getting the HQ financed and having a young son and a wife who had left St John when she became pregnant. The loyalty to your own Division is very strong and there was no way that I would have let anyone take it over, so I found myself in June looking for a new paid job, and at the same time being in charge of the Division. Bob talked Steve out of leaving and eventually, a lot later, he took on a position on County Staff as County Public Duty Officer.

There was no time to settle in, as it was the busy season. It started on June 14th with the Trooping of the Colour, where National HQ wanted a photo of some members to go on the front of the new book. The photographer took a picture of Del Boy and Jayne Signorelli while sitting in the front of our ambulance, so not only was Weybridge in the book with a picture of me at Notting Hill but also on the cover. The following day was the Sandhurst Half Marathon.

The next weekend saw the Weybridge Carnival, then the next, us on display at the Ambulance Rally held at Windsor Safari Park, where our mobile was the star attraction. We took fourteen cadets plus adults in the unit back to the Safari Park for the cadet day at the same time. The biggest laugh was Kate explaining what the sea lions were up to when the cadets watched two of them making love. She was doing all right telling the younger ones that one sea lion was pushing the other one along until one of the older cadets said, "No they not, they're shagging." This was followed by the whole Cadet Division standing by the display pool where the killer whales and dolphins were, and getting totally drenched; they loved it.

Next day was the Brooklands Reunion where we collected another £250 from the blanket collection, and that was June.

There was still no time to take in what had happened as in the first week of July we were on duty at the Guards open day at Pirbright. The next Sunday we had our first visit to "It's a Knockout" at Imber Court at Esher, where we covered it as a duty and also put in two teams of cadets who had to climb over and under and though all types of obstacles and water; they got wet again. Then we were on duty in London at the royal wedding of Prince Andrew and Sarah Ferguson, and finally to Bexhill with the cadets for the annual week camp. So it was not until the beginning of August that I had time to take in the changes that had occurred in my life.

My first aim, apart from finding a job by October, was to look at the make up of the Division. It had not struck me before, but the Division did not have any female representation at all. Also, there were a lot of past members who did not do any duties or even turn up for training but would be there at the AGM to give their views and criticise. I drew up a list of those who had not attended for over a year or been on duty (in those days we were charged per member for insurance by County, so I viewed it that if the Division was paying for them it was only right that they repaid it back by being available for duties).

Then I composed a "Dear John" letter, basically saying "if you have no intention of being active please let me know so that I could remove you from the Divisional paperwork." Someone must have complained to Bob, because I had a visit from him wanting to know why I had done what I had, as some of these people had done a lot in the past for the Division. I agreed with that, but I was more interested in the future then the past and I was not going to run a Derby and Joan club, and if that's what he wanted then he could find another Superintendent. I remained in charge. As for a female, I put forward Ginny Johnson as my Divisional Officer but even this was questioned by County. I had to explain that as a Combined Division there should be a female officer; they accepted it but really were not convinced.

The biggest shock was that as Steve had left so quickly there was no handover and I had not been shown how to run the Division. All I got was a box full of paperwork and County did nothing to help either. Talk about being dropped in it; all County did was to send me letters or ring up complaining that I had not done this or that.

August saw a very wet Notting Hill with us sheltering under umbrellas to watch the parade, but this in turn did me a favour. One of the other units was from St Pancras' Division and the Superintendent was Iris Bundle, who I had known for some time, though I did not know that she was the manager of the training centre at London District HQ at York Street. While at lunch with her I said that I would like to learn how to teach, mainly my Division and the public properly as I felt that it would be nice to do it professionally. She told me that they ran courses at York Street for people like myself and asked me to give her a ring the following week. So the next week, I contacted her and booked myself onto the forthcoming course that was running over four weekends. Having attended these and having just scraped through the assessment, it was Iris that talked me into a career change to becoming a trainer, working for London District, teaching commercial courses. I would work there for the next ten years, but that's another chapter.

As for duties, all the usual events were covered and one new one was taken on, the Met Police Mounted Horse Trials that was held at Esher. This was a cross-country event, but the best was Stock-car racing which would last until 1992 when the building of a bypass closed it down. We were never short of members to attend even though we had to leave the HQ on a Thursday by six thirty p.m. to allow time to get there, and after a while found out that if we got away at ten o'clock we could just get back to HQ and then make it to the "office" (now the "Old Crown" in Thames Street) for last orders; we even rang in our orders if we were tight on time.

One night though in our hurry to get to the "office" we did not realise that Caroline had gone to the toilet and got locked in the HQ, and only realised that she was missing when she turned up at the office, not a happy bunny.

Due to the type of duty, we had a meeting with the other Divisions, the organisers and area staff on what we should wear and some training on how to extract racing drivers out of the different type of cars. True to form, St John left it to us to arrange; in fact we covered the event for months before it got arranged. As for uniforms, after a discussion we all went for white overalls as they could be seen at night when we were on the track. Supplies introduced yellow overalls but the price, and the thought of us looking like a flock of canaries convinced us to stay in cheap white ones.

Apart from the club house, the circuit had two covered stands plus our first aid room; the rest was opened to the elements. The oval race track was tarmac with a criss-cross track in the middle for the occasional figure of eight race. We had it all, from banger racing, stocks, super stocks, vans, cars towing caravans to even, one night, Reliant Robins racing.

We had a good understanding with the organisers. If a driver was injured, a red flag would be waved and we would make our way on the outside of the track, between the public and the racing track, then through the crash hawsers; these were three two inch thick metal cables that stopped the cars leaving the track.

These caused us our first problem as we had not practised what we would do if we had a stretcher case. Well we did and we tried to slide the casualty though the middle and top hawser, but unfortunately he was rather large. In fact he had a big stomach which got stuck between the hawsers. We had to prise the hawsers apart and take him back out and then over the top one.

Injuries ranged from minor and major cuts and burns, to quite a few broken arms; these were caused when the cars crashed into the uprights and the drivers arm got caught in the steering wheel as it spun. I can only remember one broken leg in all the times we attended, and as the Cambridge Military Hospital was only a mile away, we would take the injured driver ourselves.

My first trip to the Cambridge was an interesting experience. As we unloaded our patient people kept saluting me as I had three pips on my epaulettes; it's not that easy to return the salute when you are pushing a stretcher.

It's funny how one remembers the silly things that happened at stock car. One night we had a driver semi-conscious and trapped inside and as we tried to maintain his airway with his helmet being forced down by the roof while they tried to cut him out. We smelled something burning, then suddenly Caroline who was with me leapt up; she had been sitting on the hot exhaust -- one burnt bum to treat. Another time the stock car had taken down the overhead lighting, so it was quite dark and I leapt onto the bonnet. Unfortunately, it was missing and I ended up straddled across a rather hot engine.

I have a dislike of treating eyes and one race night we went out to a super stock that had just pulled up without any apparent incident. On arriving, the marshal just pointed to the hole in the metal mesh that covers the windscreen aperture that protects the driver. Looking at the driver, the screen that covers his eyes on his helmet was broken, and as I looked inside one of his eyes was just a mass of blood. I thought "Oh my God, he's lost his eye!" and then he took his glove off and with his finger, lifted up his eye brow and his eye was still there. It turned out that a spark plug had been on the track and had been flicked up by the car in front and split his eyebrow which had fallen over his eye.

One of the oddest incidents occurred one summer evening when after arriving in glorious sun, we suddenly had a short sharp downpour of ten minutes and it became quite windy. About an hour later I received a radio message from the pit crew asking if I could go over there as they had a problem.

On arriving I was told that one of them was acting odd, Theresa Kelly or TK as she was known, was an eighteen year old and an ex-cadet. The crew had noticed that she was not taking any interest in watching the racing and was ignoring everyone, so I asked her if she was alright. At first she totally blanked me, not even looking at me, then when I asked her again she told me to F*** off. I had never heard her swear before. Shortly after this she started to slur her speech and when I went to hold her arm I realised that she was soaking wet and freezing cold. She was taken straight to the first aid room were her mother Ella was on duty. TK did not even recognise her mum and she ended up in hospital. It transpired that she not eaten since lunchtime and it had only been a snack. As it was a hot day and she was only dressed in bra and pants under her overalls, when it had rained, she had got soaked and with the wind chill had developed hypothermia.

At about the same time as we started stock car racing, the demand for our services at Queen Mary Sailing Club was reduced due to them training more rescue crews to save money. However, we were still needed for big events like the Bloody Mary where our expertise on the water and land with first aid was required. So it looked like we would have some free time on Boxing Day, but that did not last long as the stock car people had a large racing event on that day and wanted us. As my mum said, "Another door?" Even better, now we would turn up with tinsel and wearing Father Christmas hats on the day and we were dry, and for the next six years that's where you would find us. This also had a spin off, as us three Divisions would go to each other's social events, and Cranleigh's fancy dress parties were something else.

Seeing Del boy driving a minibus dressed as an elephant was something to always remember. In fact, one night, we had to stop at an accident -- poor casualty what must he thought as a St John mini bus stopped and out got Tigger, Humpty Dumpty and a spider saying "It's alright, lie still we are first aiders." Oh happy days.

While we had been at British Aerospace with the unit on display in the autumn, I had noticed that they had a E-reg transit ambulance sitting by their surgery unit, and on enquiring, found out they did not use it anymore. I wrote asking if they would like to sell or donate it to us as we could put a tow bar on it and use it to tow our boat. Guess what? In December, they donated it to us.

The year ended with New Years Eve being quiet, apart from when some yobs, while fighting, tried to get into the ambulance; nothing that five van loads of police could not sort out.

****

1987 got off to the usual start with the "Bloody Mary", but this time it was snowing and had been off and on all week, but it was still held with an air temperature of -1 degrees C and with the wind, an overall chill factor of -15 degrees C. We were crewing our boat and two others for the race; this made a total of seven safety boats all told. I was with Del boy and although we were all well protected from the elements, guess who got hypothermia -- yes me. I was wearing a wet suit, with a windproof sailing suit plus gloves, hat, even ski goggles; I had a hot meal before going out on the water and felt I was ready for the forthcoming event. As we left the pontoon, I was steering. We headed into the wind and waves and within minutes I was covered in ice as the water froze onto me. Del had it all over his back but once we were away from the shore we stopped being swamped. About half an hour later the tops of my legs started to feel really cold, then I started to shiver a lot. In fact, it got so bad I could not stop it. Then all of a sudden it stopped and then I felt quite warm, to the point that I took one of my gloves off and tested the temperature of the water; the water felt like hot bath water and I even said to Del that Thames Water must have heated up the reservoir. Daft, I know, unfortunately he did not hear what I said due to all the noise and I had a scarf over my mouth. The next thing I knew was I was watching a sailing boat sailing vertically up the horizon and I was totally amazed by the crew's skill in doing it. In fact, I had fallen over sideways in our boat and this gave Del a clue that maybe I was not well – hypothermia -- bless him. He wrapped me up in a sheet of bubble wrap and retuned to the club house. I do not remember what happened next, though I was later told that I was assisted to the showers in the changing rooms, and some one had offered me a brandy but Del had told them that that was the wrong treatment for me, then drank it himself. I came round sitting on the floor of the showers still in all my sailing gear under a spray of hot water, wondering how I had got there. Out of all the crews on the water that day, I was the only one to get it, though why, I don't know.

It took a couple of weeks to get over it fully. Even at work, two days later, if someone left the door open and I caught a cold draught I would start shivering. Still I could now teach people what hypothermia felt like, and what to watch for.

In March, while driving past the Thames Water depot at Ashford, I noticed a Land Rover Ambulance sitting in the compound but everything was locked up and no one was around. I mentioned it to Del and the next day he rang me at work very excited, asking me if I could get a letter to them as there was a good chance we could have it. Not only did they donate it to us, but they fitted a new battery and tyres as they had perished with age, and gave it a full service and a MOT.

It turned out that it was built in 1967 but it had only done three thousand miles and was only used at treatment plants when needed, and transported on a lorry between them. With a grant from Walton Charities we had it re-sprayed and put into our livery, and now we had an ideal towing vehicle for the boat. Weybridge was getting a reputation for collecting ambulances and garaging was beginning to get a bit of a problem.

Though we had attended the Head of the River race for some years, this year we got to cover the Oxford and Cambridge boat race as it was held before the Head of the River race for the first time. Due to the boat race, we could not launch at Putney where we normally did, so we launched at Quentin's Sailing Club just by Barnes Bridge. On retrieval, I was standing in the water and mud, getting our boat onto the trolley when I turned. Unfortunately, my lower leg did not, as my foot was stuck in the mud and my knee twisted. At the time, I thought that it was just a sprained/twisted knee but time was to prove me wrong.

Years later I started to have troubles with it and eventually ended up having it x-rayed at hospital. They informed me that my right knee looked like a knee of an eighty year old, and as I was only fifty that was not good news. On the upside, they did tell me that I was too young to have a knee replacement.

But having lost our duties at Queen Mary's, I thought that our boat would not be in much demand this year; how wrong I was. The local rowing clubs had seen us around both on the water and in the local press, and next thing I knew, requests were coming in from Walton, Weybridge, Staines, Egham and Sunbury rowing clubs to cover their regattas.

Also, Brooklands Museum Trust approached us to cover their events at the museum throughout the year.

About this time, we had another boxing night to raise funds for something I had in mind. Our HQ front door opened straight into the hall and during the first winter, if anyone opened it we lost all our warmth. A porch would be the answer. Secondly we were short of space with our vehicles and I was looking at adding an extra garage on the side which would possibly mean buying an extra bit of land.

April saw the release of the book "A Century of Service to Mankind" and it had been worth all the running around we had done with the author. Also, we had an informal visit at our HQ from the Chief Commander, Major General Peter Leucher CBE, who while there, presented certificates to our cadets and a Grand Prior's badge to Nursing Member Jennie Godfrey.

We were in the same location as usual for the London Marathon; the Isle of Dogs. We were inundated with casualties and ended up treating six hundred and fifty two. Thank goodness they were all minor and they just wanted to carry on to the end.

While on duty in June at a Children's Party in Hyde Park, which the Queen was visiting, I had my claim to fame. Actress Sally Ann Fields sprained her ankle while walking around in high heels on the grass and I got to treat her.

The annual blanket collection at Brooklands brought in over £420. Then it was on to Clapham Common for the Capital Radio Reggae Concert. July saw the return to Brooklands of a VC10, then it was another "It's a Knockout," with our cadets entering a team followed by a week later going to Bexhill camp for a week's rest?

One of the first duties in August was covering one of the new regattas, which was interesting. It was a two-day event with a large charity fair on shore on the Saturday and a children's regatta on Sunday. The first aid on the Saturday was supplied by the Red Cross and on Sunday, as it was a much smaller affair without the crowds we also covered the land side.

Notting Hill saw yet another location for us -- Tavistock Crescent which is between All Saints Road and Portobello Road; we were told that all we had to do was drive in. Due to the size of the unit, I even asked at the briefing a week before, whether the access would be big enough for us, and was assured there'd be no problem.

Del and I went and drove up there to check and saw that there was a locked barrier across the entrance. So we contacted London HQ and they said it would be opened when we arrived. The first problem that greeted us was that we had to reverse the unit over five hundred yards down a narrow passage onto the piazza. Getting there we found that the barrier was still locked, no one had a key. The police thought the Council had one, they thought the Fire Brigade had one, and they in turn thought the Ambulance service had one. After an hour, we were still kicking our heels, and those that know me know that I don't suffer fools and idiots gladly. In the end a police unit arrived with a pair of bolt cutters. Then a discussion developed about whose responsibility it was to damage council property. I was getting seriously hacked off by now; in the end we cut the lock.

Driving onto the location you could hear the paving slabs cracking under our weight. Still we were on station, but by this time I had missed the morning briefing (I was also Station Commander). Eventually Derek Fenton arrived to apologise for the cock up with the keys. After a tea and the usual bacon sandwich, (we were famous for our bacon sandwiches and chocolate cakes,) Derek informed me that in case of trouble all units had been given an escape route. Unfortunately, where we were there wasn't one, so it was look after ourselves, and with that he departed to visit other stations.

Sunday passed off reasonably quietly as usual, so we returned the following day complete with our own bolt cutters; thank goodness the gate was still open and with more cracking of pavement slabs, we were in.

Having attended Notting Hill now for over eleven years, I was getting very good at judging the distance that people might throw things from so that I would park her just out of range. However, I could not have anticipated seeing in the distance some "gentleman" with a long piece of plastic drain pipe. As I watched, his mate loaded something into the rear of it and then he pointed it down the road toward us and the police.

The next minute I saw a large rocket suddenly leave the pipe on its way to us. I yelled at everyone to get down and the rocket bounced on the roof of the unit and then disappeared into Portobello Road. A police riot squad went flying past us as they chased the culprits. We then settled back down treating the now continuous flow of mugging and stabbings that were brought to our station. At about ten o'clock p.m., there was a general broadcast to evacuate, and as I looked up into the night sky, I saw the twinkling of bottles being thrown. I made my way to a doorway of a nearby property and facing the road. I had learned years ago that if you faced the bottles at least you could parry any that were heading your way; if you tried to run, getting a smack on the head or in the back could do a lot of damage.

I had to smile though, as when I had yelled "incoming," two of the triplets from the division had run and tried to get into the unit's front door.   Now the front door only allowed one person in at a time and as these lads were quite large they nearly got stuck in their panic. Afterwards I overheard Elle Kelly telling them, "Look, the time to panic is when you see Ray run."   I thought that was nice.

Due to the history of our unit, in September, we were invited to a Bus Rally taking place at Woburn Abbey and we were one of a hundred and seventy-six buses that were on display that day, and many people who had travelled on her in the old days of Across Trust came on board to look around.

With all that had happened before, nothing could have prepared me for the next duty though. It was the usual four days of golf at Wentworth, and the unit had gone in on Wednesday. I had been on duty on Thursday and left it all locked up safe and sound. It was the 15th of October and during the night there was the big gale that savaged all of southern England causing an immense amount of damage. Strangely both Kate and I slept through the gale and it wasn't until I turned the radio on and then the TV did we realise how bad it had been.

Still, I thought at least where the unit was parked she would be safe as there were no trees near her. Then came the problem of getting the ambulance from Weybridge. Due to all the trees that had fallen, it took me over three quarters of an hour to get to the HQ, then when we had enough people to crew, we set out for Wentworth.

Luckily we came across a tree surgeon who cut a way for us through the fallen trees, and we arrived to find our lovely mobile unit covered with a tent. It was not a small tent but a part of the tented village that was on site, and included scaffold poles. The blue lights had been smashed off, a window was broken and there was lots of damage to the paint work. But by lunch time we were operational and they had even started to play golf. Yet another insurance claim for me to fill in with "Who do you hold responsible and what speed was the other vehicle travelling?" etc. At the HQ, the gale had blown down loads of conkers, so a conker championship was organised for the cadets and became a regular event.

But trouble was brewing. Kate had been told that her Junior section would have to be closed down by the end of the year, as a new unit would be launched (Badgers). She fought against this as a Junior's age was from seven to ten and the Badgers age group was going to be five to ten. She felt that the age gap was too great, and this came to a head in December when she was ordered to disband her twelve-strong Junior unit. She was also getting very disillusioned with the fact that it appeared that only males were being recognised by the Order of St John, and after fourteen years of running a very successful Cadet and Junior section, and attending many major events in London she felt she was being overlooked. This was made worse with certain people being made Serving Brothers, despite the fact that they were running their Division into the ground.

Finally in June, she resigned her role as Divisional Superintendent of our Cadets. When she was told that she would be transferred to County Pool so that she could carry on doing duties and retain her rank, her first reaction was "That's where they put people out to grass who are no use." In the end she did transfer into it, but the seeds of discontent had now been sowed. Still, at least we still could go out together on duty as our son Neil was at university and Sam had left home to live with her drunk of a boyfriend. These duties included London Theatre shows and the Royal Albert Hall that we now covered.

Then three years later came the final incident, attending an event with Ginny Johnson at the Royal Albert Hall. They were treated with rudeness, hostility and resentment by the other London District members that were also on duty there. Even a steward there asked why she had been spoken in such a rude way. Kate came home and promptly wrote a letter to St John World (our magazine) about this incident. She said if she was a new member and was spoken to like that by people that were badly dressed and grumpy, she would leave and join an organisation that did not resemble a Darby and Joan club, finishing the letter with "Yours, but not for much longer." Within a week of it being published she received a very caustic letter from a County Staff Officer John Smith, saying that he did not buy the St John World to read such a letter and was insulted to be referred to as a member of a Darby and Joan club. Well if the cap fits wear it.

Kate promptly resigned after eighteen years, and from that day had a total hatred for anything to do with St John and referred to it as "that dreaded cross." This was really the beginning of the end of our marriage, as not only was I running the Division with all the work it involved but as I was also training for St John in London District, it was my job too. It paid the mortgage and gave us a reasonable lifestyle. Many times after a row I would offer to resign, but she knew that it was my life and that if I did, things would only get worse. So we really did not have much to talk about now, and with her now working as the PA to the Head of the Inspectorate of Police and not allowed to talk about her work, home life was not pleasant, To anyone outside of home, it seemed as though everything was all right. Thank goodness though, when she resigned from cadets we had some one to take over -- Jayne Signorelli, an ex-cadet herself, still it would be seventeen years before Weybridge had a Badger Sett.

****

1988 started with a new member contacting me. Mark Hover had just moved into the area and wanted to transfer to us, from Croydon as he knew all about Weybridge. He became a life long friend of mine, and still is. He held the rank of Corporal at his old unit and as I did not have one at the time carried on in that role. He also sailed.

In the spring, County had a request from Thorpe Park Leisure Centre to man their first aid room. It was discussed with the local Division and a rota was worked out between the Divisions who wanted to do it. Initially it started all right but after a couple of months problems started to occur. The first I knew about it was when I was told that they had been instructed to wear the uniform of the park as they did not want St John uniform being seen there. They also did not want ambulances being called, but if they were in fact necessary, the casualty was to be taken to the back entrance, as ambulances were not to be driven to the first aid room. It finally came to a head one Saturday. We were supposed to be there only 'til five o'clock and on this day we needed to leave on time to go back to our HQ, as we were on duty at stock-car racing at Aldershot by six thirty. At quarter past five, Ginny took the keys back to the office, and was told she couldn't leave as the park had still got people in it. Ginny pointed out that our agreement was up to five o'clock. Then she was told "You will stay, as you are like any casual staff and will do as you are told." Ginny raised two fingers and left. When I heard about this I checked with the other Divisions and found that they were having similar troubles. We all pulled out of the duty.

In May, the cadets were awarded the Lady Osborne Shield for the Division whose cadets had done the most number of duty hours per cadet. With Kate resigning from Cadets I was very lucky in that Jayne Signorelli took over She ran it successfully for the next four years until the demands of work, and finishing her D of E gold award forced her to stand down.

While at York St, I had got talking to Monty Levie, who was in charge of theatre duties. He was happy for us to do any theatre duties we fancied, subject to booking with him, as they had problems in getting them covered. Leisel Flusser was in charge of the Royal Albert Hall (RAH) and was also having the same problem with cover.

Though neither of these duties paid, I looked at this as a reward to my members for all the work they did. Leisel was a lovely person; she looked hard and severe but to us, Weybridge, she was a joy to know, and would leave us in charge of an event and have a evening off. The RAH had a good size first aid room, with stretcher bays all screened off, and a treatment area; the only trouble was equipment always seemed to go walk about. When a performance was on we had to have first aiders at either side of the arena and stationed by some of the aisles as well as the first aid room, and if we had enough members, a couple up in the gods. In theory that meant a minimum of ten people.

As we started attending the RAH we also did the last event at Earls Court. This was a George Michael concert, followed by the opera Aida, then I believe the organisers supplied their own first aiders, though there were rumours that it was also due to St John not being able to supply the numbers of members required by them. Whatever the reason, it was the end of our involvement at Earls Court. But now we had the RAH and what a choice of events. Leisel died of cancer following a period of illness. A lot of us from Weybridge attended her funeral and not long after that the RAH organised their own first aid cover.

Some of the Performers I saw at the R.A.H. between 1988 and 1995 included Ella Fitzgerald with Count Basie's Band, Frank Sinatra, The Hollies, Harry Connick Jr, Mike Oldfield, Sting, Tony Bennett, Dionne Warwick,

Barry Manilow, Richard Clayderman, Randy Crawford, James Last, Phil Collins, Spinal Tap, Kitaro, The Shadows, Simply Red, Eric Clapton, Tom Jones, The Monkees, Liza Minelli, Sammy Davis, Frank Sinatra and the Who, in a performance of Tommy.

As a rock and roller and Heavy Metal fan, the next list was a bit lost on me but we still had to do the good with the bad! Some of this was wasted on me personally. I saw the Bolshoi Ballet, The Proms, some operas, brass band concerts, school proms etc. And of course there were non musical events too, like Miss World, boxing, and tennis events.

Recalling some of these artists brings back certain memories. When we were booked for Kitaro, the first remark was "Who? Never heard of him." A violinist's not really my thing, but how wrong can you be? Before the start of the show we had the usual casualties coming for help, you know "Have you anything for a headache?" "I've a blister on my heel", "I've grazed my hand when I tripped over" etc; the only thing was when we filled in a report, they had come from Canada, Brazil and Spain and all over the world just to see this man, and they raved about him. So when the performance started I went in to see what it was all about. The best way to describe it was a cross between classical and Led Zep. He played an electric violin and huge drums mounted vertically; it was very impressive.

I always, when in charge, would make certain that everyone on duty would see part of the show and not be permanently stuck in the first aid room, though there could be the odd time where we would draw straws for who would go and watch the event. This usually occurred during the Proms season, as Leisel had instigated a system to stop people just turning up for the good duties. For instance, with The Last Night of the Proms, everyone had do attend a minimum of six proms, and some of these could be dire. Once on this evening, four St John personnel turned up that were not down for the duty, and had not done any of the Proms. Leisel promptly read them the riot act and sent them home. Mind you, you should have seen the look they gave us as we were from Surrey.

One of the "Last Nights" the conductor was seriously ill, and was likely to die that night; they even flew him in by helicopter. Leisel asked Del Boy and me to be the stretcher party so that in the event that he collapsed and died, we would rush out and load him on it and take him back stage. As the whole thing was live on BBC TV I raised the question about should we not be resuscitating him and what about the cameras? It was well organised. If it happened the cameras would pan up to the ceiling and the person sitting at the side of the stage was his personal doctor and would pronounce him dead. As it turned out he survived and died two days later, all Del and I saw of the nights performance though was on a nine inch black and white monitor we watched back stage in the dark. Another time we got into trouble on "The Last Night" was when we brought our St John flag with us so that it could be hung over the front of a box as flags of all countries were often displayed on the night. We asked a group of people in one of them if we could and they gladly said yes. Someone from the organisers took umbrage over this and ordered that it should be removed. I don't know why. Anyhow the people in the box refused saying that they had paid for the box and they would do what they wanted to. Quite a row blew up but in the end it stayed, and was seen on TV that night.

The Who played "Tommy" one evening with Phil Collins and Billy Idol and others guesting in the show, and at the end, The Who were banned from giving an encore as down in the basement they were measuring the vibrations on the support pillars and it was causing damage. No wonder I have slight hearing problems, but again what a show!

Eric Clapton would book RAH every year in January/February for seven days and play to a full house each time, but it's the other things that happened that I remember. Once we had a young man who was in a wheelchair and had a terminal brain tumour, and we were looking after him. Somehow Eric Clapton found out about him and he was invited back stage after the show to meet him. What a nice man. He talked with him and gave him some personal bits and pieces and made that guy's day. My daughter Sam and I were at one of the concerts the year after his young son had died after falling out of a fourth storey window to his death. He seemed to be showing his sorrow through his music and when he played "Is there a God In Heaven?" you could hear a pin drop and at the end fans were crying, including Sam.

As usual, if anything seriously happened at the RAH we seemed to be the ones on duty. Del and I ended up doing resus on the steps outside when a large gentleman, about eighteen stone, collapsed and died of a heart attack. Another incident that always sticks in my mind was at the Christmas Carol Concert. Two of us responded to a call to a young woman who had fainted up in the Gods. Just as we arrived, the lights went down and the show got underway. So there we were in the dark, with the chairs at an angle and of course she had to be in the middle of a row, lying down between the seats. A quick look using our torches showed that this was no faint. Her eyes and mouth were open, and she was not breathing! Initially I started to try to do CPR, after sending my colleague to get help, both 999 and others to give us a hand. Trying to do it at an angle in the dark in the confined space was proving impossible so with help I decided to lift her over the seats to the exit. What a nightmare. First, we had to move the people who were sitting there. I still can remember her head banging into the tops of the seats; all this was happening while carols were being sung. By this time a stretcher had been brought up in the lift to us, so she was loaded on to it and transported down to the first aid room. I carried on doing CPR while all this was going on.

It turned out she was a thirty five year old and to add to the problem, her two young daughters were with her and came down to the first aid room. We organised one of us to take them outside and look after them, while Kate and I carried on working on her. This was the days before Bag and Mask and Oxygen; this was basic street first aid, so Kate and I worked together just swapping mouth to mouth and chest compressions when one of us started to get tired. Bear in mind we still had to cover the event so the others were on their stations. We kept going, and for the only time ever I experienced a horrid situation. As I blew in I heard a bubbling noise, and just as I went to blow in again she vomited into my mouth. Now I don't mind blood etc; but vomit is not my favourite. This started me off, so now I was doing CPR as I was vomiting over her; what a mess. We grabbed a few triangular bandages and carried on blowing through them until the ambulance arrived, which did seem quite some time. In fact the crew's first remark was "Sorry about the delay."

They quickly checked her out and after a couple of tests said "She's gone." I knew that, I said, but we were not allowed to stop and also we had her children just outside. So they took her but had me doing CPR just for the children's sake, until they loaded her into their ambulance. My guys had organised transport and contacting their father, so that the children could be taken to hospital. We all returned to the first aid room to clear up, do the paperwork and have a debrief. Someone brewed up, but when I went to pick up the cup I found I could not stop shaking, and had to drink it with a straw. When we went to find out the time of when the ambulance was called for our paperwork, we were amazed to find from the initial called logged by security to when it arrived was just under forty minutes; we had to resuscitate for over forty minutes. No wonder the crew had said sorry; we found out later what had happened. The first ambulance responding to the call had been T boned at a road junction and rolled, injuring the crew and the other people in the car, so with that needing at least three ambulances, ours took a long time to get to us. As we were all just taking in what we had been through, there was a knock on the door and in came a little girl with her Mum. "Could we have a plaster for my daughter's finger, as she's cut it?" Back to reality.

Months later I received a letter via Leisel from the husband of the woman, thanking us for all we did for his wife, and though she was only thirty six, she had been born with a defect in her heart and had been a walking time bomb but no one knew it. The only thing that could have saved her that night would have been a transplant. But he said at least she had not died without people caring, and his children would always remember how we had tried to save their mum. It was ages before I could forget that night, and I have never eaten McDonald's since, as that was what she had had that night. One other funny one though was when I was called to a man "not feeling well" and on arrival found him sitting propped up against a wall. As I approached him I had already diagnosed heart troubles, as he looked ashen and was having breathing problems. I used my usual opening remark of "Hello, my name's Ray. What's the problem? Where's the pain?" He informed me he had no pain, no numbness, and no pins or needles; in fact no signs or symptoms apart from a shortage of breath. But when I took his pulse, what a pulse it was all over the place. One minute it was 160 + then it slowed down to 40 then it started to miss a few beats, then it went screaming upwards again. While waiting for the ambulance to arrive that I had already sent for, I asked him had if he'd had this before. His wife answered in a Somerset accent, "Oh yes my darling. He's had about five of these turns in the past few months." I asked her what the hospital said, and she said, "Oh my dear, we didn't go to hospital as he got better." When the ambulance arrived they informed me that I was dealing with a silent heart attack; his sixth? In all the years I had been doing first aid, and teaching I had never heard of it; another new thing I had learned. That's what I like about first aid -- you are always learning some thing new.

As well as the RAH we had also had the chance to see London shows and for the next three years we could pick and choose whatever we liked. I saw to name a few, Starlight Express, Me and My Girl, Miss Saigon, Blood Brothers, Aspects of Love and rocked and rolled in the aisle to Buddy more than once.

While we were attending all these, we were still attending all our local events of rugby, fetes, Brooklands

Museum, Regattas and local sporting events, and every year the demand for our services increased. Another first was our attendance at the International Air Show at Biggin Hill, and with my love for aircraft I was in seventh heaven, and then to make my year a request from London District -- would I like to attend two days at Docklands Area for Pink Floyd concerts.

Would I? They may have been sixteen years older, greyer and fatter, but their music was as good as ever, and the audience was made up of all ages, from people like me that saw them back in 1973 to youngsters who would not have been born then. On the first evening, just as the second half started, Del and I got a call to return back to the first aid room. They had an unconscious drugs overdose, and as we were experienced in dealing with this type of casualty they asked we take him to hospital. Well, we loaded him but I made the mistake of leaving him unbuckled after adjusting his position. Suddenly, after about five minutes he came round, and I learned afterwards he thought I was a two-headed eight flippered penguin that was attacking him, and he attacked me. I was now yelling for Del to stop and give me a hand. He stopped and I saw him running away. I started to think all sorts of things about him, but in fact he had seen a police car and the next thing I knew was the back doors were flung open and three burly police officers piled in and restrained my patient. By the time we returned to the concert it had finished; thank goodness we had next day to see it all and I told them that we were to be the last ambulance to be used.

After attending the Notting Hill briefing at York Street, and having been assured that the gate would be open this year, it came as no surprise that it wasn't, but this time we were prepared -- we now carry a pair of bolt cutters, another lock destroyed, hee-hee!

Then, an unusual request on the Sunday – could we supply an ambulance and crew to cover the test match as London District had been let down, and as Sunday was quiet, I delegated the role of station officer to Mark and had a change of scenery. Still saw England thrashed by Australia.

November 5th was a bonfire night duty, at the Met Police building at Imber Court, Esher. It was a huge display requiring the unit and both ambulances, and once covered is now a regular duty booked on the night for the next year. We also had another boxing night as it was our fiftieth anniversary of being formed and this seemed a good excuse to do a bit of fund raising, and put Weybridge in the middle of the action again. The action was at the Lord Mayors Show when a police horse bolted and ran into the crowd, injuring six people.

As I mentioned earlier, we now covered rowing regattas on the Thames from Egham to Molesey. All but one were the usual type of rowing with eights, fours, pairs and singles. These events were races against the clock and each other and were very competitive. Sunbury Regatta was different; this was a fun event with a large charity fair on shore with all the local charities having stalls and a beer tent etc, all held on a large island in the Thames. The racing was in old style two seated rowing boats with some other races on punts. These were called Dongerla races and local groups dressed up in fancy dress and would kneel, paddling the punt Indian style and trying to steer it, usually without much success.

On the Saturday evening, there would be a large firework display to end the day. Sunday was a quieter event; a junior regatta, where the course was shortened and only under fifteen year olds would race. This also gave the organisers the time to break down all the tents and equipment from the day before.

After the first year (1987) when the Red Cross did the land side on the Saturday, we turned up in 1988, after launching at Walton Bridge and travelled up though Sunbury Lock to be greeted with lots of people waving frantically from the shore. The Red Cross had failed to turn up, and as it normally attracted over three to five thousand people they had to have first aid there. So we were asked if we could help at all. Ten minutes later and after a few phone calls, I had managed to find a couple of my guys who would collect an ambulance from the HQ and come over.

It transpired that the Red Cross had closed down in the area but no-one had informed or returned the regatta's request for first aid. From now on we would cover the event on land and water, and still do twenty two years later.

In all the years of attending, I can only remember about four times we had rain. It is a standard joke between us and the organisers that the sun always shone on them. Only once did the event get cancelled, and that was a junior regatta where we were asked our opinion on the condition and they used our advice to call it off. Most of the first aid incidents occurred on land and mainly on Saturday and would consist of wasp strings, cut fingers and feet often caused by walking in the water to cool off, though we did have one serious incident when someone climbed up a tree and then fell out. On the water it was very rare that we had much to do apart from pulled muscles and knee injuries.

The biggest problem for us was that on the island, there was access to the main road via a foot bridge and through a ford, but on the other side of the river it was only a tow path with no access at all, so if we had any one injured there we would have transport them across to the other side. Also the race course was just upstream of Sunbury Lock and some of the driving skills of people who had hired a boat left a lot to be desired. Also it is not illegal to be drunk in charge of a boat, and putting alcohol and water together in this context is a bad combination as the next incident shows.

The last thing you would expect to treat on the water at a regatta would be a fractured spine, but this was exactly what happened at one of the Saturday events, and of course I had to be on duty; this time not with Del as he had left by now, but with David Stevens.

We were just patrolling along by the towpath when a Dongerla slowly passed us to moor up before the next race. They were a bit merry, and they sprayed us with water from the water pistols they were carrying. I made the comment to them "Just you wait till you're injured, I'll get my own back," but as it was a hot sunny day we did not mind, and it was all in good humour. As we returned from the end of our patrol I saw someone standing on some rails on shore about ten feet above the punt doing a Titanic impression. The next second he fell and I thought that he had gone down between the punt and the concrete wall. Knowing that it was over fifteen feet deep, and if he had struck his head he would be in troubles. We powered up to the incident, every one was yelling and screaming, and then he popped up in the water laughing. Now we realised that we had a casualty on the punt, when he had fallen he had landed on top of one of the female occupants.

She had seen him coming down and leaned back, if he had landed on her head and she could have sustained a neck injury. Instead, she had severe pain lower down in the middle of her back, and to add to the problems she was a bit merry, and vocal. We stabilised her in the punt with cushions and with someone immobilising her head, we lashed the punt to our side and very slowly crossed the river to the island. We had already radioed the land team to call Surrey Ambulance and get our ambulance to the shoreline so that we could offload her and have her ready on a long board, collared and ready for transfer. As we moored up, it struck me we had never practiced this scenario, a spinal on a punt on water; this was going to be interesting. As we were stabilising the punt and to be honest trying to work out what we would use to get her off the punt, a young woman came up to me and said "Can I help? I work for the London Ambulance Service?" After what happened years ago I ask her to prove it. She could. In the end we used a scoop stretcher to get her out of the punt and on to the long board and by the time Surrey turned up she was ready to go and still being very vocal. I learned later that she had sustained damage to her spine in the lumbar region and spent over six months in hospital, but did end up being able to walk with a stick.

Two and half years later I had to fill in a report for lawyers as she was suing the Regatta organisers for allowing her to drink, but seeing that she was part of a team from one of the local pubs, I was not surprised that I heard nothing more about it.

3

THE LATER YEARS (1990 – Present)

1990 was going to be our last time in the docklands for the London Marathon; just to show our ability we treated six hundred and fifty seven runners. I sometimes wonder whether we get moved because where we turned out to be the busiest, and some one got jealous. Still, London District asked if we would like to go to the Chelsea Flower Show. Great -- only I think I found out for the first time in my life was that I suffered Hay Fever. I didn't do that duty again.

Another new event came from Surrey; the Pepper Harrow cross county horse trails. I'm not a horsey person and even the Derby bores me apart from the casualties we have to deal with, but at this event a horse fell and broke it's leg and though they put up the screens around it, we were on the wrong side. As we were dealing with the rider, I witnessed the horse being put down. It's odd that I can deal with injured and even dead people but I cannot touch or watch injured animals. Also another first when I was called by a vet to a horse that was stationary and did not react to anything. The vet informed me that he had seen something like this before and did we carry any oxygen as that was what was required, though he said it could go either way either the horse would recover or drop down dead. We made a mask out of a plastic bag and got the rider to get ready on her, then 100% at 15 litres, within a minute its ears pricked up and then it took off like a rocket with the rider hanging on for dear life. It worked. We even got to cover Polo at the Guards club at Windsor.

A request from County HQ saw us getting stuffed up with a transport job. "It's only taking a man to a home for respite for his carer." We told her that the charge was £50 and she would have to be happy to do it." Clive Huggins was a thirty year old who we learned, had been knocked of his push bike by a hit and run driver ten years earlier and had suffered serious head injuries leaving him permanently disabled. He had been studying at an art college and was still painting. He was in a wheelchair for most of the time and it took quite a while for us to understand what he said. Mrs Huggins was a lovely little old lady and how she managed to lift him and look after him was unbelievable, but she did. What we found out when we arrived was that the home was in Southern and Mrs H, as we got to call her, was under the impression that the £50 was for both trips and as we could see that she was not wealthy and did not get any support from social services, we (the Division) decided not to worry her. For the next two years we took Clive to Southend and he then went to a change of venue at Hatfield, which meant we would go right round the M25 as Hatfield was exactly halfway round.

Clive started to bring his electric organ with him and would entertain us with his playing, and after dropping him off Mrs H would sleep on the way back. After another two years at Hatfield and we had another venue, Southampton, overlooking the Solent. This place was lovely and then after two years it suddenly stopped. We no longer received any calls from her. Whether he had got too much for her and had gone into a home, or she had died we never heard.

Notting Hill came round again, and yet again another bolt cutting exercise, still this year we had a guest; Surrey Commander Dr Tony Blowers who wanted to come out with us but did not want London District to know. He just wanted to work with Weybridge and even did his share and made the tea.

September was the fiftieth anniversary of the Battle of Britain. We were stationed on the Mall on a very hot day. As usual, I missed the fly past as we were busy dealing with lots of faints etc. We also got involved with covering events at Shepperton and Halliford film studios. They were recording Red Dwarf and a couple of adverts at Shepperton, and we got to meet the stars of Red Dwarf, and Russ Abbot who was filming a lager advert. He was very interested in knowing why we were there, and when we explained that it was for him, in case he got injured as they were using flame throwers, he was amazed that we were volunteers and wanted to know all about St John and us and made certain that we went for meal breaks with his crew.

At Halliford, they were making Pampers adverts and because there was a baby on set they had to have an ambulance there. This was because while filming in Germany a baby had fallen off a table and had died. Neither Ginny nor I enjoyed these, as they filmed the advert back to front. When the baby was tired and wanted to go to sleep and crying, that's when we inferred the baby was wet and needed changing, and after it woke up this was after the nappy had been changed. It was amazing that if a nail needed knocking in, it had to be a chippie to do it, if a light switch had to be switched on it had to be an electrician. Ginny asked if had to stir her tea or was there a man there to do it for her.

1990 saw the first issue of the Surrey News, the brainchild of Geoff Francis, who had to fight to get it off the ground and Weybridge, was one of the first contributors and would appear in every one from thereon in. We also recorded the highest number of duties we had ever done in one year to date – three hundred and thirty seven.

1991 and yes, back to normal -- the Bloody Mary. The event started cold but sunny, with forty five minutes remaining to the finish a force ten gale crashed through causing all sorts of trouble.

The London Marathon saw us back at the finish, but parked round the back of County Hall in Jubilee Gardens. Needless to say it was very quiet apart from the damn tannoy.

A memorable duty was Pavarotti in the Park, where the great man sang to a sea of umbrellas, in Hyde Park. It rained and rained all afternoon and evening and there were people selling black bin liners at a £1 each. The only casualty was a man who had been attacked by an old lady he had complained that her brolly was in his way and could not see the stage, so she hit him over the head with it.

Four new events were attended this year, the first was a St Thomas' Summer Ball at Cobham, where lots of very drunk medical students did some really silly things, but it kept us busy. The second was motor bikes on a scramble course at Lyne next to the local tip. Those that use the M25 will know the smell when you get to the M3 junction; thank goodness the duty only lasted only six months, though they had to be the hot summer months. The third event was the RSPCA open day at Chobam

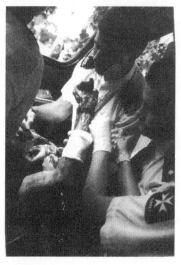

which was really a pleasant duty; I even got chatted up by three bunny girls, much to the amusement of the guys on duty. The fourth was in November when we had passed to us by Guildford Division the Holmbury Boy's Firework display, because Guildford had so many displays to cover and we were free that day -- we have covered it ever since.

Notting Hill resulted in us receiving a letter of praise from the London Ambulance Service saying that due to the excellent work done by us and the paramedic, the patient had survived. it happened on the Monday afternoon, as usual I was Station Commander and about four o'clock, I looked up to see a police officer running towards me and pointing behind him. Four police officers were running carrying a person between them, each holding a limb and leaving a trail of blood on the pavement. I just yelled "Incoming, serious bleeding." They dumped him on to the stretcher bed and three of our team grabbed anything that was pouring blood. As they rolled him over to see the extent of his wounds I could see his rib cage and a lung. As a Station Commander you must not get involved in treatment, so apart from giving my guys equipment, I then called for a paramedic as I could see we would have to stabilise him on our unit before he could be moved. While this was going on Chris Dunsmore said "Quick, take a picture of him." Well, I got a couple of shots off and then the paramedic turned up and all four of them worked on him. I found out he had been attacked and stabbed then thrown through a shop window, hence the wounds. Talking to the paramedic afterwards, he reckoned that he was high on drugs as though he had lost a lot of blood he still had good blood pressure. They put at least two litres of fluid in him before he was moved. We had to replace all three white shirts of the team as they were covered in blood.

Brooklands Museum held a MG owners picnic day, which caught them out as over seven thousand people attended. This caused a traffic jam right back to the M25 at Ripley. During the afternoon, a young boy came up to me and asked if he could have a couple of plasters. I asked him why and he told me his sister had fallen on the test hill and cut her leg. I asked him to bring her down to us and he told me that she could not walk. We went to her to find she had an open fracture of her lower leg. At the end of the day the usual blanket collection netted over £1,000. Other events at Brooklands included "Fly In" where light aircraft would visit on certain days, landing and taking off later in the day on what was left of the runway. We would park with Brooklands Fire and Rescue by the control tower, and made some good friends with them. In fact Paul Swift joined us from them, which was quite an asset as he held a HGV licence and also RYA certificates, so in one move we had gained an extra mobile unit driver and a safety boat coxswain.

Also, this was the start of blue lights being knocked off by our garage door, Ginny Johnson becoming the first to suffer before we solved the problem. Because of this and other incidents I decided to have a presentation on AGM night for a bit of fun, as it's always good to have a laugh at oneself.

1992 saw the first. Ginny was presented with a cake in the shape of a blue light covered in blue icing, made by Chris Dunsmore who was a chef. The following year Jayne Signorelli received a cake in the shape of a clock complete with a clock face. She had put her clock back instead of forward when British summer time occurred, and turned up two hours late for a duty. Jayne won it again a couple of years later when she should had ordered twelve triangular bandages, but unfortunately ordered twelve packs of twelve so we had a hundred and forty four; a cake in the shape of a triangle was presented that year, and so it went on.

We also had a caption competition; a picture usually taken by me would be pinned up on the notice board inviting members to add a comment; some of these were brilliant.

****

1992 was a year of extremes. Derek Fenton retired from his role as Commissioner of London District after many years, and we were ask to attend his official leaving do, and being his "marauders" we jumped at the chance. It was held on the Mall and we presented him a chocolate cake as he always took one up to London duties for us, usually made by my wife. This one was inscribed with "End of an era." He was one of those special men. If he said stand on your head you would; you would never question it. He was a first aider first and not a social climber. I would have followed him with the Division to hell and back.

All this moving our unit around at the marathon was not down to him, but others who bowed to pressure from people who did not want Weybridge, an outside Division working on their patch. But we were a tried and tested unit with a lot of experience.

On the way to the Derby, as we came into Epsom a lorry coming from the other direction drifted over and our mirrors collided, the first I knew was a bang and I was sprayed with broken glass, poor Ella Kelly who was sitting on the offside, (remember the unit was left hand drive) was peppered as the mirror had come through the door glass. Luckily neither of us was seriously hurt, though we both spent the duty finding glass in our hair etc; and when I got home and had a shower you would be surprised where I found glass particles. We had to wait nearly two months to get a new window, though we made up a temporary one out of Perspex. This at least made us operational, and so we attended Biggin Hill air show, where we had something different to treat. Towards the end of the duty we noticed that a couple of haystacks were on fire in a farm at the end of the runway. Just as we started to stand down and put everything away, a soldier was brought in with smoke inhalation from fighting the fire. We put him on oxygen and after a while he improved a bit but not as he should, so we called over a doctor who told us to take off the oxygen and he would be alright and walked outside. Of course he wasn't; we put him back on the oxygen and called in the doctor again, who again told us to take him off it as he didn't need it and walked off. By now I was getting very cross, so I told the doctor that as we were ready to go we would send him in to hospital as there was no-one to take him. Finally he went in still on oxygen. As I didn't know the doctor I was chatting to him afterwards. I asked him where he came from and what did he did in the NHS. He was a St John doctor from Oxford and a Gynaecologist; no wonder he was no good at treating our soldier.

At golf at Wentworth in October, a well-known golfer saw a snake sunning itself on a rock. He then poked it with his finger whereupon it turned round and bit him on it; it was an adder. Though we dealt with the patient, one of my young members told a Sun reporter that he didn't know what to do with a snake bite; you can imagine what appeared next day in the Sun newspaper. November also saw the last meeting of Stock-car racing at Tongham due to a bypass being built through it. It was also my birthday so my guys had a record played for me "Hawaii Five-o." Yes, it was my fiftieth. Jayne Signorelli had to stand down from running the cadets due to finishing her Duke of Edinburgh Gold award, and another member, Mel Carter took over

We were back on the Isle of Dogs for this year's London Marathon but only treated a hundred and two runners as they had us stationed up a side road, but it was better then being at Jubilee Gardens. A rather unusual duty was an end of film party at Shepperton Studios. The film "The Muppets" where we had them all there, dressed as Kermit and his gang. But the highlight for me was the change to the HQ building. I had already knew that we needed more garage space but also as the meeting hall's door opened straight outside, in the winter all the heat would disappear, let alone the security aspect. In the end we purchased a little bit of land next to us and had an extra garage built that would house the safety boat and the Land Rover, and a porch at the front which also not only kept the heat in but gave us the extra security. Also, we got rid of the stones in the car park and had it tarmac all over, at a total cost of £25,000.

The number of duties attended in the year was down to three hundred and three but that was still an average of five a week; not bad for a Division of thirty five members.

By now we were beginning to struggle with vehicles for covering events. There was also a change occurring in the request for our services.

In the seventies most of our duties were a 20/80 in favour of London but by the eighties it was about 50/50. Now in the nineties there were more and more local events needing first aid cover, and it was more like 98/2 split.

Instead of the London Theatres, we were now at the Yvonne Arnaud at Guildford and the Peacock Centre at Woking on a regular rota. Also, we were on a rota which allowed us to work at the A&E at Ashford on a Friday night, and some of us were even were invited to help on some Saturday evenings. The problem with ambulances was solved when I remembered that Woodham and Byfleet Division had ceased to exist, though it had not been officially closed down, and knew they did have an ambulance, and after pleading our case to County HQ, Bob Hutton was told we could have it. It was a Bedford CF with a Wadham body on it and a chrome bell under the bonnet, but it would do sterling service locally before it ended its life at an ambulance museum two years later.

1993 was to prove to be the busiest in record with the Division attending three hundred and seventy one events, though Simon Eyles, my Duty Officer's own unofficial target was four hundred, but we have never achieved that number before or since. My daughter Sam who had married that boyfriend in 1988 finally Divorced him this year and then a couple of months later fell of a ladder while pruning a large bush in her garden and broke the same arm that she had when she was small. This time though she did not keep quiet about it. I received a call from a neighbour telling me she'd had a fall, and I arrived just as the ambulance arrived. I did not know Sam knew so many swear words and after being put on entonox and loaded she told the crew she was worried about how to pay her mortgage. I loved the remark the attendant said, "Don't worry Sam, that's what Dad's are for". Sam did not waste her time while out of action, she wrote "Ode to the Bow Tie" which was printed in the St John magazine and was a caustic comment on the bow tie that was then part of the uniform; in fact a year or so later it was dropped.

It seemed that I was attracting drama at this time, as later that month I was teaching a first aid class at the HQ and BBC were filming it for an hour as a back drop to one of the BBC 999 programmes with Michael Burke. Right in the middle of it one of the students said "I don't feel too good, I'm sorry" and had an epileptic seizure. The film crew thought it was staged and even remarked what good acting it was until they realised that it was for real.

The London Marathon saw us back in our old position on the Isle of Dogs and we treated two hundred and two runners. We also took our mobile unit to the Guildhall as the Across Trust had the latest model, the Mk XVI on display, and wanted the old Mk I to be there as well. It was a lovely day with so many people wanting to see what we had done to her. The Derby was its usual self apart from when an old gentleman was brought in with what appeared to be burns over his arms and face. It turned out they were mustard gas burns from the First World War which always came up when it was very hot weather. Talking to him I found out he had joined up when he was only fifteen, but this still made him over ninety years old although you would not have thought it. He refused to go to hospital and said to me all he wanted to do was rest in the shade and could we just treat the burns with cold wet dressings, and would it be alright if one of my nurses could put on a couple of bets for him. How could I refuse an old soldier and Mel even won £74 herself from his tips.

When he left, he thanked me and said "God willing see you next year young man." Young man? Not bad to be called that at fifty.

In July I had a new member join, an American, Sharon Forrest, our first foreigner who got the nickname of the mad yank. She was great and once we had worked out that the sidewalk was the pavement, and the car lot meant the car park and a few others, she very quickly fitted in to the Division.

We seemed to be a magnet for film crews this year. We had a film crew with us at Notting Hill this year but did not have anything dramatic for them and we then covered filming for three days at Brooklands Museum were they were filming a 1920/30's period story with a lot of motor racing. September saw a visit from the Commissioner-in-Chief and we put on a display on the river with a mock rescue at Walton Bridge for him.

Due to the amount of duties, we had our annual flag day moved to November where we had the best collection ever with us collecting a record £990. Whether this was due to the publicity we had during the year or the change of month I could not work out.

Back in the early nineties, we'd had a request from London to help with Crystal Palace football matches and on our first duty met a lot of our old colleagues from Bexhill camp, now adult members including Chris Dunsmore the custard pie thrower. (See appendix 1)

Chris, who was working at Woking started to attend our meeting nights as well as his own Division and also came out on duty with us. He said to me once how he was so impressed with our training and how did I get the members to practice basics so often. We did resus every six to eight weeks as his Division refused to do it.

This attachment became permanent in 1994 when he became engaged to Sam my daughter they then in 1995, went to St Lucia to get married and on their return I organised a party for them, even flying in her brother from Australia as a surprise to her and her Mum. Earlier in 1994 we attended the London South Eastern Dinner  Dance, which was held regularly in November of each year and was so impressive that at the next Superintendents meeting, I suggested that Surrey should do something similar. What a negative response. One comment from Walton was "You're wasting your time. I tried it and no one was interested" and apart from two other Divisions all seemed anti and said it wouldn't work. Well no-one tells Weybridge that it can't be done. A committee was formed of four people (not me as I was having a few problems at home and at Division) though I needed to be kept informed as it was Weybridge's money being used.

So the Surrey Dinner Dance came into being, though it started as the Western Area Dinner Dance run by us but people thought that it was a fundraising event for Weybridge and were reluctant to support it, so we changed the name a couple of years later to the Surrey Dinner Dance, and informed every one that it was a no-profit event and was for a general get together for members and friends.

The first dinner was held at the Oatlands Park Hotel the following year and we had eighty people attend, which was not bad for the first attempt and at least it broke even; this was the start of the annual dinner dance and we remained at Oatlands for four years only moving when they put up the prices. The next venue was the Woodlands Hotel at Stoke D'abernon which was another excellent hotel, but again after another four years and a change of management and price we again moved to the Hilton at Cobham.

We are now well established there and now in the fourteenth year. Last year, 2008, one hundred and forty people attended at the Hilton at Cobham, not bad for a "no-one will be interested" do.

****

1994 saw St John instigating the new rules regarding driving and crewing ambulances; Level 1 – crews for non urgent cases, and Level 2 for emergencies, i.e. blue light work, and also to assist the national ambulance service. Up to now we just did it, and it was down to the Division to train their members in what they thought they needed. With our contacts we managed to get trainers and paramedics from LAS to teach us, and had been doing so

for quite a few years, but now it would be official and certificated though it would not be until 1995 that it would be implemented.

1995 was the year I met Jane, at Hammersmith and she joined us in March.

I was also made an Officer Brother of the Order, and finally solved the problems of the ambulances by purchasing two second-hand LDV ambulances to replace our existing ones. Though identical to look at both inside and out, one was a diesel and one was a petrol engine, and the only person to make a mistake with the fuel was me. I was refuelling one day and was explaining to a new member, Diane, that one had to be careful when filling up between the diesel and the petrol one and promptly put a gallon of diesel in instead of petrol much to her amusement. I topped it up with a full tank of petrol – I got away with it but we did smoke a bit for the first few miles.

Our London Marathon station was in the usual place, but the main events for the year were the fiftieth anniversaries of VE day in May and VJ day in August, both were held in Hyde Park and the weather was beautiful; both very hot sunny days. Due to the length of the duty, London District had decided to issue everyone with a different colour badge so you could only work for eight hours and then you were supposed to go home. I asked what we were supposed to do as we could not go home and also they had me down as station Commander all day. They gave us all three colour badges each.

They say you are never too old to learn and certainly this happened to me on VE day. At midday, I had sent half of my team to lunch and with a foot patrol out on walkabout, it left only three people on the unit. A young man informed that his girlfriend was not feeling well and asked if I could go and see her. I suggested that she came back to the unit as she would be out of the sun and cooler, and after a bit of discussion she reluctantly came on board.

She was a twenty year old, who was looking very pale and sweaty with a pulse of 110 and fast breathing, so I laid her down and raised her legs and began to question her. I went through it all -- are you in pain etc. She informed me that she had a dull ache in her lower abdomen, and she'd had it on and off for a week or so.

She had made an appointment for the coming week with her doctor, and this led to the question as to whether she might be pregnant. She replied with a very emphatic NO. I ask her about her period, but it was not that, so maybe it was what she had eaten. When, what and how long ago? Had she been keeping up her fluid intake? Yes. Had she been sick? No. Taking her pulse again, I was surprised that it had got worse and her colour had not improved.

At this stage I was running out of ideas. I even suggested that it might be her appendix. "No chance" she said; it had been removed a few years earlier. You name it, I asked it; nothing made sense. So I radioed control and had her sent to the field hospital were there were a couple of doctors working. As luck would have it, one of them I knew was a gynaecologist. Later on in the afternoon I had need to go over to the field hospital for some equipment and bumped into him, and as I hate not

knowing what is wrong with a patient I asked. Well he asked me what I had asked her and what checks I had done, then what did I think was wrong with her and said "Come on you, must have some idea." I said I did not know and that's why I had sent her to him, then he smiled and told me that she had an ectopic pregnancy, and if she had left it any later she would have died. Thank goodness her boyfriend had made her seek our help.

Notting Hill was yet another hot weekend and on Monday, our first interesting casualty was a young woman from New Zealand who had been swimming the night before and had fallen over and had split her head open in a swimming pool. As she was drunk she had left it to the next day and it was only when her mates saw the unit they thought she might need seeing to. Well, this split was over eight inches long and the top of her scalp with her long hair moved around like a bad fitting wig. I asked if there had been much blood loss but she could not remember. She went to hospital. Later on that day she returned to thank us, and proudly showed us the thirty odd stitches she had in her head.

Later on in the afternoon I was standing outside the unit with Jane, one of the new members. It was her first time at the carnival and I was just explaining the do's and don'ts when I noticed a West Indian woman walking towards our unit and even remarked that her red blouse did not match her orange coloured hair.

As she got nearer, I realised that her red blouse was from her own blood. Someone had slashed her on the top of her head -- another one to hospital. As usual it was a quiet Sunday and a busy Monday with all the muggings and stabbings that unfortunately occurred at this event.

In the autumn, on the annual trip with Clive Huggins to Southampton, Jane was unusually quite and I asked what the matter was, and after I said that it's better to talk about things then to bottle them up, she told me that her twin had just told her she was gay and had a girlfriend. I said, "So what," as my son was gay and had either of them suddenly changed and grown horns or something. He was still my son and I loved him dearly. After what she and her sister had gone through together as kids, did it matter as she was still her sister? Jane was amazed about Neil as she did not know and agreed that I was right.

1996 turned out to be a year of change, and what changes. First it was becoming a drag driving into York Street. I worked out that I was spending nearly fifteen hours a week in traffic and it was getting worse. I asked if I could only work at Kingston and Feltham as this was so much nearer, a request they tried to meet. I did not mind driving to London Uni though as the pay was considerably more and the courses were so enjoyable to teach.

By June though, I started to look at possibility of teaching for Surrey as they were using my HQ at Weybridge as a centre and it would only be a ten minute trip. As luck would have it, Mr Ralph Brown was in charge of Surrey Commercial Services and I had worked with him when he had trained in York Street to be trainer. I also knew him from the days of stock-car racing, so from August I changed over and then worked for Surrey St John. The longest trip was to Guildford occasionally -- a whole twelve miles away, though I was sent to the Royal Botanic Gardens at Kew once. When I queried about it being in London, I was told by Ralph that it was shown as Surrey in his incredibly old map, though the map was dated 1895. Well, ok then.

Surrey St John had a much more relaxed atmosphere to work in, with a more flexible attitude to making the course fit with what the customer required. For instance at Kew, they were all gardeners and wanted to know about treating injuries that could happen there, the only problem I had was they were used to working outside and it was a cold spring. Due to the heat in the classroom, they kept nodding off, so I had the heating turned down and the windows opened and I taught the course wearing gloves and a coat. I was freezing and ended up with a cold; still they gave me free tickets to go to Kew.

A new duty started this year, first aid cover at the Ambassadors Cinema and Theatre complex at Woking. This was done on a rota between the local Divisions and meant one could see either a show or the latest film as there were five cinemas and two stages.

This year saw us moved to the Mall for the London Marathon. This was not the finish but the nineteen mile point, and we treated two hundred and sixty runners as it was a very hot and sunny day.

Unfortunately, life at home was becoming uncomfortable with more and more rows between Kate and I about St John and other things. At the same time, I began to realise how much I had in common with Jane and also learnt that her marriage was also in trouble.

The final straw in our relationship occurred when I went with one of my members to do a transfer to Stoke Mandeville Hospital. We had received a desperate request for us to move a casualty with a spinal injury from Hammersmith Hospital to the Stoke. When we arrived the mother was so grateful, as they had been waiting three days to get her moved. With hindsight we should have never been asked to do this transfer. The young lady concerned had an unstable C7/T1 fracture and was paralysed from the chest downwards. They could not give us a nurse escort as it had not been asked for, and we could not arrange a police escort even though we asked the LAS.

The young lady was twenty-nine and had fallen down the stairs at home late at night and had laid there until the postman heard her shouting for help at ten a.m. the following morning. It turned out that this hospital transfer had already been cancelled twice before, and with her mother pleading with us we agreed. Sitting in the back with her, travelling at about fifteen miles an hour, this was one of the longest trips I have ever done. I learned that she was a solicitor, and was due to get married later that year and her fiancé was an airline pilot. I know that I can talk, but what do you talk about for four hours to someone who will never walk again, whose whole life as just fallen apart, and is the same age as my daughter?

Despite all the years I had done in St John this job deeply affected me, and the drive back was in total silence. When I arrived home, Kate went mad as I had said I would be out for the morning but due to the nature of the job got back at seven o'clock in the evening. Once you lose the ability to communicate in a marriage it's all over, and it was. Jane and I then became an item as they say and when Kate challenged me over this and asked if I was having an affair I told her I was. I was thrown out of the house there and then.

An ex-member of Weybridge, Les Blake came to my rescue as he offered to put me up in his house while I tried to sort out my life and still run the Division, though the latter probably kept me sane. I stayed with Les until Christmas when I found some where to stay. Jane and I finally moved in together the following April when she bought a lovely house in New Haw.

1996 would be our last time attending New Years Eve at Trafalgar Square. With all the new regulations in place in the last few years it had become a very quiet duty. The fountains were boarded up, no bottles, cans or spray cans were allowed to be taken into the square and the numbers were restricted; this year we only treated one casualty, a St John member with a headache. With all this control, trouble now often occurred in Leicester Square, Piccadilly and all around the area. Our ambulance was kept busy but we were not. This led us to decide to have a party at the HQ on New Years Eve, instead for the following year.

1997 turned out to be our last year at the London Marathon. The organisers had changed the route and now it finished on the Mall, and we were at the end, a bit of déjà vu? Again the weather was extremely hot but for some unknown reason bottles of water had not been delivered to the finish in enough quantity for the runners. Instead, someone had ordered that it be left out on the course. It got so desperate that they limited the finishers to just one bottle each, which was totally inadequate for the conditions. We ended up with St John organising water trucks from Thames Water to the finish to alleviate the problem.

Then yet another new event; the London to Brighton Bike Ride. In the past the Red Cross had covered this event but this year we were asked to, from London to the finish at Brighton. So London District, Surrey and Sussex were all involved. Looking at the previous year, it showed that three heart attacks had been treated at the first aid station on top of Ditchling Beacon in Sussex, so Weybridge was sent there. It was a good job Jane knew the area and she told us that the only way for us to get there was to go to

Brighton and then onto Ditchling as the unit would not get round the bends. Not only that but to be on station by seven in the morning with the roads closing at six in the morning, the only logical thing was to go the night before and sleep in the unit, which we did.

We treated lots of riders that day and not one had a heart attack, although we did treat a rider with an open fracture who came from, of all places, Weybridge. We are now in our twelfth year of covering this event.

Yet another event was Jazz at Guildford which was the forerunner of Guilfest. But the saddest duty of all was the funeral of Princess Diana. It was rather poignant that having been on duty at her wedding, I was now on duty at her funeral. On account of the expected crowds, we were stationed at Whitehall from six p.m. the evening before, covering right down to Westminster Abbey. Someone brought a large candle which was lit as soon as we arrived. At about four in the morning we started to get casualties, mainly children suffering from mild hypothermia; parents had brought them with them and did not realise how cold it can get that time in the morning. Having now been on duty for over fourteen hours I was not in the mood for some of the comments made by St John members turning up at eight o'clock from other Counties demanding tea, coffee and to be allowed to pick a place to see the cortège. They were very firmly told that they would do as they were told and if they did not like it they could go home.

Whether it was all the stress of the lead up to the funeral or not I don't know, but about a fortnight before I noticed that I was developing an odd heartbeat, just every now and then it would miss a beat. After the funeral it got worse, but being a good St John man did I tell anyone? Of course not, not even Jane. Matters came to a head a fortnight later when teaching a four day course at Weybridge. On the second day it had become a lot worse with now an odd fluttering feeling in my chest, so I rang the doctors and was told I could have an appointment next day. I explained that I needed it today and was given one for the afternoon. I then rang Sam, who was heavily pregnant, to see if she could cover my training for a couple of hours that afternoon. Next I received a phone call from Chris at LAS control where he worked on the phones, telling me to ring for an ambulance right away, and if I did not he would send one from London as he wanted his unborn baby to have a granddad when he came into this world! That made me dial 999 straight away. By this time I was even picking out who in the class I thought could be good at CPR on me.

Sam arrived and then Surrey Ambulance who hooked me up to a heart monitor and read what was going on with my heart. I was a bit worried when I heard one say "Ooh, that's different" as my heart missed a double beat," then they told me that I was not having a heart attack but they had never seen a trace like that before and asked if I could I produce it again. I told them if they waited a few minutes it would do it again, and it did! It was so embarrassing being wheeled out past my class of twelve and then on to the A&E at St Peters in full St John uniform.

Sam had contacted Jane who worked in London. She was on her way but would be at least an hour before she could get there. In the meantime they started to do all sorts of test, took a lot of blood and did an ECG, then there was a long wait and by this time Jane had arrived. The doctor who was dealing with me returned. The good news was that it was not a heart attack in any form. Then he asked me if I was under any stress at all. I said not really apart from the fact that I had left my wife at the end of last year, I was still supporting her financially with the mortgage, and trying to get her to Divorce me but she would not hear of it. My son had informed me that he was HIV positive, and my daughter was expecting my first grandchild and was due very shortly. Sam was only four years younger than Jane and was having difficulty in excepting her as my partner, and I was running a very hectic St John unit and having a problem with one of the members.

At this he said "Stop! Not under any stress? You must be joking!" He then told me to take some time out and relax, and asked if I had any hobbies? "Yes," I said, "St John and fishing." Well I was told to take a few days out fishing and I would find that my heartbeat would settle down as it was being caused by chemicals released by the stress I was under. Well you live and learn. He was right as well. After a week of fishing it all returned to normal.

A week and a half later I was in Exeter teaching for Davies Wine Bars. They had bought a couple of hotels in Devon and wanted me to teach the staff the type of first aid course that I did at their London branch but over two days. Jane and I went and stayed there and made a short holiday of it. A phone message on the first day informed me that I was a granddad. Alex had been born and both he and mum were well.

Even in Exeter, I still managed to find some first aid to do. We were walking down the High Street when we came across a young man who had fallen of his push bike and was having a seizure. Having sent for an ambulance we both dealt with him, and it turned out his doctor had changed his medication and this was the third one he had had this week. Though he did not want to go to hospital I convinced him to go so that they would check why this had happened.

In November, Jane and I went to Cyprus for a well deserved two week holiday. It was wonderful -- no phone calls, no duties, no St John and no heart problems; just what I needed -- a complete rest.

****

1998 started with our usual rugby events at Vandals rugby club, but then we found that their large tournament clashed with the London Marathon date, and when I put it to the members they surprisingly said they would rather do rugby then the marathon, as they were fed up with smelly feet and getting up very early to get on station; also there was better variation of injuries at rugby and besides all that it was our local duty.

By now life in the Division had settled in to a regular pattern of major events -- Golf at Wentworth, London to Brighton Bike Ride, Derby Day, Guildford Jazz had now been renamed Guildford Blues and Pop festival before becoming Guilfest, then Notting Hill followed by golf again in the autumn, firework events on November 5th, and of course all the other smaller local duties.

We had two new events for 1998 – firstly, a two-day international Paint Ball competition near Fetcham, and secondly, a trip to Sussex for the Goodwood revival weekend.

The only major thing that happened to me this year was while on duty at Brooklands Museum was another brush with nature. Nearly all the events we covered there were either fly-ins with real aircraft or events with lots of old cars going up test hills, with the associated crowds. Then we had a request to cover a model aircraft club flying display. I should have known better after my experience back in the 60's but to be honest my crew mate (Adi) and I thought it would be a boring duty.

We had parked about ten metres from the static VC10 aircraft to cover the model flying display, and just to add to our boredom it started to drizzle, then dark clouds started to build up on the horizon and slowly came our way. These now became black, and I must admit we both commented that we had never seen clouds that black before. Then we heard the rumble of thunder and even discussed where the heart of the storm must be.

All of a sudden there was an almighty bang; the ambulance seemed to leap up in the air and then crash back down to the ground. Now everything seemed to happen in slow motion. I watched lightning run all over the VC10 and then jump off. One lightning bolt struck the commentator of the display and I saw a blue light jump from his face to the mike that he was holding. People who were standing holding umbrellas suddenly collapsed as the lighting struck the metal tops of the umbrellas. There was blue lightning running all over the ground and one large bolt of lighting jumped from the tail of the VC10 to the metal bridge that crossed the River Wey. It then ran along the top of it before jumping into the museum building.

There were people lying everywhere. We jumped out of our vehicle and started to check them all, and unbelievably they seemed to be alright. The commentator had a minor burn on his nose and hand but was more worried about his radio equipment and insisted on carrying on with the show.

Fifteen minutes later, we had a call from the museum. One of their people had been struck by lightning and though to begin with said he was alright, was now complaining of burns on his hand and pain on the sole of his foot. On checking him out, we found he had the classic entry and exit burns of an electrocution and was dispatched to hospital. If anyone ever asks me to do another model aircraft display I will decline!

1999 started of with the sad news that one of our ex-cadets had died in the Philippines. She was working for a Voluntary Overseas Aid group, teaching young children, and while swimming had been caught by a rip tide and drowned. Her mother contacted us with the news and eventually presented us with the money to buy two pulse Oximeters (machines to measure patients pulses and oxygen levels) in her memory as she had enjoyed her time so much with us.

The highlight of the year for me was the birth of our first son, Jamie, in May. He came in to this world weighing 9lb 4oz (ummmm is that heavy for number one compared to my Sam & Neil?)

We had attended numerous boating duties in the first half of the year but I was surprised that while on duty at the Staines Regatta in July, one of the organisers remarked that he had heard that all St John boats were off the water. This was the first we had heard of it. Then another club rang us up to enquire whether we were back on the water yet as they were arranging their regatta soon and needed to know our availability. We even covered this event (Sunbury), but by now I was getting worried and started to make enquiries. I asked County HQ if they knew anything, and the answer came back no but they would contact National HQ (NHQ); that produced a quick response. It transpired that someone had been killed in February while training in London and ALL boats had been taken of the water until further notice and a board of inquiry had been held, as well as an inquest.

NHQ had no idea which counties ran boats and had notified Cambridge St John about the order -- well I suppose Weybridge and Cambridge sounds similar, though what Cambridge must have thought as they did not have any boats at all I have no idea, so now we were off the water until whenever.

Later on I received a request from NHQ to sit on a board to set up a new code of practice in relationship to safety boats., with one other person from Weybridge. I took Paul Swift with me as he had a lot of experience of working on rescue boats out in the Mediterranean The first meeting was quite interesting as we had representatives from all Divisions. This included the Welsh, who did offshore work, Rutland water, (basically on a large lake with no current to worry about covering sailing events), Lake Windermere, who covered high speed power boat racing, and Reading, who like us worked on the Thames. There was also another Division that covered events at Bristol docks. One Division from Humberside caused the lawyer with us to nearly faint when he was told that they covered offshore power boat racing and they also would Dive into the sea to rescue any driver who was trapped underneath an upturned boat.

The accident that had caused the problem had happened when London District had an open day to encourage new members to join, and while taking a university student out on the water in a safety boat. An incident had occurred and he had died, and though no one had broken any regulations as such, the regulations were somewhat vague and did not cover the diverse situations that we all operated under. Also, St John had been fined by the Health and Safety Executive for lack of care.

After three meetings, a new set of regulations were drawn up that covered day time, night time, tidal and non-tidal, offshore and on shore activities. Out was the swimming training in your pyjamas in the local swimming pool; I could never understand why, as we all wore sailing suits and buoyancy aids when out on the water, and as for rescuing a brick from the bottom of the twelve foot end of the swimming pool?

On the Thames you could not see more then six inches and with all our equipment on you could not Dive down anyway. This ended our involvement with London District Tideway Division as we were now not allowed on tidal water. Our operational range stopped at Teddington. Before then we had worked just past Tower

Bridge, but we would have to wait until the following year before the legal boys had finished with the final draft.

1999 would see our last involvement with Notting Hill for some time, but then yet another new duty started in September. St George's College requested first aid cover for their school rugby matches. These took place every Saturday afternoon from September to December. The request came from Runnymede Division as the college was just in their area but they could not cover every match. It started with us attending one a month as we had our own rugby to cover as well, then it became every other Saturday followed by three a month, finely at the beginning of November, Runnymede said they were unable to commit to any and we then took the duty over completely.

***

Early in 1999 Surrey Ambulance Service (SAS) and St John Surrey agreed that St John would assist them on Friday evenings and a rota was drawn up for us to work for them. At the beginning we transported non-urgent casualties to and from local hospitals. On arrival at our HQ at seven in the evening we would ring SAS to find if they had anything for us to do and we would be available until midnight; well that was the theory but if you were given a job at eleven forty five by the time you had dealt with it and returned back to HQ it could be more like one to one thirty in the morning.

My first ever job for them was a job that had been waiting since five o'clock and was a doctor referral. Then the location was given as Pratt's Bottom. Fearing a wind up, we questioned them, but yes it was real. The next question was where was Pratt's Bottom? We were told it was near the Dartford Tunnel, and at this time of day it would take a good forty five minutes at least to get there, but we were informed that we were the only unit available, so off we went and did the job.

Finding the local hospital more by luck than by knowing the area, we finally got back at ten. At the beginning it really depended on who was on Control whether you were given any jobs, as some Ambulance Controllers were very against St John working for them while others were quite happy to use us. There was one in particular -- if he was on you knew that you would not stop all evening with jobs; we liked him. Certain Surrey Ambulance crews on the road also had a problem with us working, and more then once I was given the two finger salute by passing vehicles, but as time passed we ended up with a good friendly working relationship apart from a couple of local crews who could still not forgive St John for working during the ambulance strikes of the eighties.

At the end of the year, the work then extended to responding to 999 calls, either backing up other crews or working independently and calling for assistance if required. More then once when asking for back up we were informed there was none available -- "You will have to deal with it on your own." With us now driving to incidents on blues and twos it was decided that the crews should have a driving assessment. This consisted of a question paper on the Highway Code, and then a hour's drive around Surrey with a SAS driving instructor, even using blues and twos as well.

I started to have doubts at this time about our involvement with SAS, as if you were in the service (SAS) the driving course you took two weeks, and we were doing just half a day. Also, it was making a "them and us" situation within the Division. Some of the members who did SAS work seemed to look down at the other members. Also, they thought that the local fetes and duties were beneath them and would not volunteer for them; even worse they were reluctant to take part in basic training. I even heard one make the comment, "Well you are only a first aider." "ONLY A FIRST AIDER!" I was furious and had a few strong words with the person concerned.

On the plus side, one certainly gained a lot of experience in dealing with incidents and casualties and the use of our equipment we carried. One night, we were called from our HQ to the Oatlands Park Hotel just up the road to a collapsed, not breathing casualty. It was a race between a unit from SAS and us. We got there first and were greeted by the sight of a waiter doing CPR on an elderly gentleman lying in the middle of a dance floor. I was greeted by "Hello Ray, am I doing this right?" He was but I wondered how he knew my name; it turned out I had taught him six months earlier. SAS had now turned up and proceeded to shock him while I used a bag and mask on him *[a hand held resuscitation device]*. The only thing the SAS lady did not say was "stand clear" so it was lucky I saw her finger just about to press the button and let go of the equipment otherwise I could have had a shock. Unfortunately he did not survive.

My last job assisting the SAS I ever did was on New Years Eve 2000 in the afternoon. Three of us were crewing -- Paul (Swifty), Rob (Mr Pipie), and me. At about two o'clock we were sent to Virginia Water to a male with breathing difficulties. Arriving, they both went into the house while I turned the vehicle around as the road was a dead end. Rob came out and his body language told me something was wrong. "What's up?" I asked. "He's dead!" Rob said. "Do you need the Defib?" "No," came the answer, "he's got rigor mortis." That's a first.

Now to speak to Control. Having stated our call sign I informed them that our patient was dead. She came back with "We were told he was having breathing problems." I replied "Well he has 'cos he can't breathe and he also has a bit of rigor." They then had to send out a paramedic to check him and the police were called because it was a sudden death. Within five minutes we had a house full, paramedic and crew man, two police and us three. (Party Time -- sorry)

Now there was another problem. We would have to wait until Control could find a doctor to come out to officially confirm death as the paramedic was not legally allowed to in those days. It seemed silly that both we and the SAS crew should have to stay there so I suggested to them that they should go as they were needed more then us and after they checked with Control, departed. We then went into the kitchen where the man's wife and son were.

It transpired that the couple lived in Wales and had come to spend the Christmas holiday with her son. Her husband had already suffered a serious stroke and was in bad health. She was a lovely lady so I just sat with her and we talked about everything, from the state of Welsh Rugby to the birds in the garden. She told me that she was so happy for him as he'd had a great Christmas with the grandchildren despite suffering badly with pain and the inability of being unable to move much due to the stroke.

We finished off their Christmas cake and chocolates and many cups of tea before the doctor arrived an hour or so later. On the way back to HQ both Paul and Rob saying that they could not believe the way I had talked about rugby with her while her husband lay in the room next door. Why not? It was better then just sitting there not talking and looking glum, and she wanted to talk as well.

It had been six years since I'd become a Level 2 *[a level of ambulance qualification]* and having renewed my certificate three years ago, I by now was very disillusioned with it all. I had joined to be a first aider, not a part time worker for SAS. Let's be honest -- it was cheap labour for them. But the peer pressure was on to be one and with so many courses that needed to be taken I wrote an article in the Surrey News, our County magazine, on why I would not be renewing my Ambulance Aid 2 certificate. Amazingly I received quite a few phone calls from members of other Divisions agreeing with my comments.

****

2000 turned out to be an expensive start to the Millennium for the Division. We took delivery of one of the new Crusader ambulances; the cost to us was £20,000, the other £20,000 being paid by County. The HQ windows were replaced by double glazed ones and that cost £6,000. Then a major blow -- our beloved mobile unit's engine finally gave up. To be fair it had done over a million and a half miles in it's life, but a con rod appearing through the side of the engine was terminal. The only answer would be a new engine if one could be found, as she was over twenty nine years old. This was left to the garage that had been looking after her for the last fifteen years. Steve (the boss) spent months looking for a replacement engine both in the UK and abroad to no avail. It was six months later when a store man in a local Mercedes lorry dealer remembered that they had an engine in a box buried somewhere. After a search they found it and though it was not quite the right one Steve could make it fit with a few modifications. The cost would all together be around about £6,000, and it would be a year before she returned to us; the cost though was met by a grant from Walton Charities.

One good bit of news was that our safety boat was allowed back on the water in July, just in time for Sunbury Regatta. I must say though, I was quite glad to see the back of 2000. The Division felt lost without the mobile unit.

2001 started with two ex-Red Cross members joining us. Annette and Richard had met at uni and also joined the Red Cross there. Having finished, they had moved into the area and at first joined a unit at Kingston, but then decided to look closer to home and turned up one night, and after seeing what we were about, joined us. We even forgave them for being in the Red Cross.

I also started to plan my standing down from being in charge as Superintendent, as I would be sixty the following year. My daughter, Sam started to shadow me at major duties and accompanied me to meetings so she knew people and they knew her.

As I have said earlier there are certain people who attract trade, they are always in the right place at the right time and like me, Annette was one of these. This year at Biggin Hill on the Saturday, one of the jet aircraft belly-landed on the runway. It was said that it was due to a technical fault; in fact the pilot had forgotten to lower the undercarriage. This was the first crash. The following day, Annette and Sam were in the unit and as the aircraft flew by Annette started to say "KABOOM" when all of a sudden there was an almighty KABOOM and THUD followed by a plume of smoke rising up in a farm field at the end of the runway; a jet fighter had crashed into a farm field killing both occupants – the second crash. After a while the show resumed and about an hour later as we watched a world war fighter going through its display, iit suddenly plunged vertically into the ground; the pilot had no chance – the third crash for the day. We had been attending the Biggin Hill air show for over twenty years and we hadn't seen one crash, let alone three. At this time, we did not know who the jinx was, but it soon came clear; it was Annette!

In December late at night, Annette had attended an accident outside her flat in Morden. A boy racer had driven into a parked van at speed and both him and his passenger were trapped -- the girl critically injured. Annette had gone to the crash dressed in her dressing gown and stayed inside the wrecked car resuscitating the girl while the fire brigade cut the roof off to gain access. She then volunteered to assist the paramedic on the journey to hospital using a bag and mask, but the girl was pronounced dead on arrival. Then in January the following year, while on a skiing holiday in France, a snow boarder crashed nearby and sustained a neck injury. Annette took charge until the helicopter arrived, then a few months later dealt with a fatality at a road traffic accident.

For her actions in assisting the paramedic, Annette was awarded the Ambulance Service Institute Public Spirit Award. Although ten awards are presented each year, only one is reserved for civilians and it was presented to her at the House of Commons in October 2002.

St John is very bad in recognising actions by its members that are above the normal call of duty. You get told that you must have served at least twelve years before you can be nominated for a Serving Brother or Sister, yet it appears to the members that if you are high up in the organisation that rules do not apply. With this in mind, I sent in a full report to County HQ asking for some sort of recognition for her actions but heard no more. Ironically I received a letter in October informing me that I had been made a Commander of the Order.

My last year in charge was memorable but for all the wrong reasons. On the bright side we purchased a new engine for the boat with an electric start -- WOW! No more aching arm muscles after a boating duty. In October, I went to St John's Gate and was invested as a Commander of St John. On the sad side, the Queen

Mother passed away and we attended the funeral, stationed at Parliament Square by Big Ben.

While all this was happening, I was involved in one of the worst events that I have ever experienced in all my years. Back in beginning of 2001, the Cadet  Superintendent had to stand down as she was expecting a baby and also moving out of the area. One of the senior cadets, aged eighteen had offered to take over, and as there was no one else available, Area management and I agreed to it. It was not until towards the end of that year I started to realise that things were not going well. A few times I asked him if he required any help either on meeting nights or with the paperwork, but he assured me everything was under control and he could manage.

The warning signs were there. There was no training programme, and cadets started to leave. Also, one night I happened to be there doing some paperwork in the office, when, in a panic, he came into see me. Area and County staff had turned up to do the cadets' Annual Inspection, but he said he did not know anything about it. I found it hard to believe that he had not been notified, and of course he had. Then I learned from them that they had not received any paperwork back from him for nearly a year. I was a bit annoyed that no-one from County had bothered to contact me about this as I always felt that I had dual responsibility for both cadets and adults at Weybridge. At the end of the year, after a talk with me, he agreed he wasn't managing and would stand down from being in charge, but would attend in January to handover everything to the new person.

Hindsight is a wonderful thing. An eighteen year old is not experienced enough to control cadets that are nearly the same age as him. Without managerial skills, any eighteen year old would struggle and also would be reluctant to both ask for help and admit that he could not cope. I asked for a volunteer at adults for someone to take over. The only person to come forward was Jane, my partner, who like me, did not want to see the Cadet Division close down.

Now I found out the depth of the problem in hand as Jane was faced with filling in the annual returns. He failed to turn up at any meetings at all. There were no records of attendance, subs or uniform deposits, and some of the cadets had not been enrolled. Proficiency subjects that cadets thought they had done during the year had not been registered and later we found all the relevant papers at the back of the cadet cupboard. It took her over three months to finally sort out the returns.

Jane inherited a glorified youth club and had to stamp her authority on it. She set about getting it back on track with a training programme and sorting out the Grand

Prior subjects and increased membership. Two of the inherited cadets nearly left as they had not received any of their certificates, and of course they did stay on and both achieved their Grand Prior's Awards a couple of years later (Joanne Swann and Fiona Howell). Another of the existing cadets was a boy age fifteen, (TTs) who had been transferred from a local Division at the request of County. We were told that the Division was having problems with him and County thought that he might be better suited to a larger one. Also, his father was an ex-member of Weybridge.

A Young Lifesavers course was registered and started, and four cadets were sent to a Cadet Leadership course in February. By the end of this month, the membership had doubled with seven new members among them being TTs younger sister (TTd). One worrying thing was that TTs &TTd's dad started to stay to "help" in the evening, but this help often turned into contradicting what Jane was telling the cadets and one evening even told her "confidentially" that he knew that the previous leader would be returning to take over again after Easter. This was utter rubbish but caused Jane some stress after all the work she had put in to sort out the mess. When she contacted County, they informed her that in fact she was now officially Member in Charge, so much for him returning!

Early in March, six new members attended a weekend Action Pack course for new members held at Ash Vale, run by Mr Peter Rubie. Jane attended this to see what was taught and transported them there. On the Sunday afternoon, while checking their uniforms, Jane was helping TTd to fit her female Nursing hat with hair grips, and found that TTd had head lice. As Jane had not received any formal training or advice from County on how to deal with anything like this, she told Peter who told all the cadets that it had been seen that one of them had head lice and they were to tell their parents. Peter also told Jane to let TTs's parents know, which Jane did on returning back to HQ. The reply from her father "What again, I'll get her mother to deal with it" and that was it, or so Jane thought.

Then on the 18th May, Jane received a phone call from Dept Commissioner Mary Boland telling her that TTs father had made an allegation against her that she had "Thrown his son half-way across the meeting room" and did she know anything about it. It was definitely not true! Mary said that she did not think it could be but had to ask, and told us not to worry as they would deal with it. Jane was very upset and in tears, especially as she had spent some considerable time in sorting out TTs Grand Prior certificates. Knowing the father as I did, from when he was in the Adult Division I knew what a devious character he was, and I advised her that this needed to be sorted out quickly.

Jane then rang the father and told him that she understood that he had made a complaint against her and it was not true. She told him to write a letter of apology or follow it up with the County's Child Protection Officer as the allegation was slanderous. He replied that he had been advised that he should not speak to her or anybody about it. When she asked him when the alleged incident was supposed to have happened, he could not remember the exact date, but said that it was a couple of months ago and he had witnessed it. Jane then asked him why he had allowed TTs & TTd still to come to the meeting evenings since, and suggested that they should be kept away until she got an apology. She then tried to ring the Commissioner, Child Protection Officer (CPO) and the Dept Commissioner back -- no answer from any of them. She then left messages on their answer phones; still NO-ONE returned her call.

Without a date, it was very hard to pin down the allegation, but Jane remembered that one evening when fitting out two new cadets with their uniforms, TTs had pulled one of the girls' hats off these had to be fixed to the head with hair grips) and hurt her and she had ended up in tears. Jane had reprimanded him in front of his father, telling him that if that's the way he acted then he would not be considered for the role of NCO in the Division.

This was the only reason for the allegation she could think of and reported back to the CPO and left it with them. I then learned that TTs, TTd and their father were now attending the nearest Division to us. I reported this to County HQ saying that the Superintendent should be informed of the allegation as our Divisions sometimes worked together. I was told not to say anything, which I thought was unfair to the Divisional Superintendent, so I had a quiet word with her to warn her as a friend.   In fact we learned a year later after all the troubles that TTs had actually been involved in another "incident" with a cadet at that Division. If I had known about at the time, I would have refused to accept him.

By now it seemed that it was this incident with the young cadets which was being used as a case by the father, and Jane was requested to submit a full report, which she did. At this time I started to get reports from parents of our cadets and other members of St John that the father was going round telling people that Jane had attacked his son and he was going to get her thrown out and then he would take over running the Division.

I spoke to County HQ about this and that he needed to be stopped but the response was basically indifference, so with this in mind I called all the adults together and with Jane attending told them all that was going on and naming names, as I did not want any of them being put in the position of some one walking up to them while on duty and telling them what they had heard. When I told the now new Commissioner, he was not very pleased and said I should have not done it.   Well tough, I had, and would have even taken it to the local papers if needed. Finally a date was set for a formal interview -- 14th of July.

Jane requested that I would attend with her, but this was denied as I was also her partner, so then she requested that her elder sister, who was the manager of Sussex Citizens' Advice Bureau would attend; this also was refused. So in the end she appeared on her own in front of the new Commissioner, the Deputy Commissioner and Bob Hutton. Worse was to follow. Instead of one allegation there were now two. She had raked TTd's head with her hands in front of other cadets looking for head lice, and when told "You are aware of the allegations" she informed them that no-one had officially told her, either in writing or verbally and this was the first she had known about the head lice allegation.

When Jane came home and told me, I was furious that someone who had been only member in charge for five months should be put through this ordeal, and then I learned that they had treated each allegation separately. Not only that, but it turned out that no-one had interviewed the two girl cadets to substantiate the event. We now had to wait for the panel to give their findings. All this time delay had taken its toll. Jane suffered health problems, with her asthma getting worse, skin rashes and time off work as well as her confidence being undermined. Finally the panel gave its report, and none of the allegations had any substance.

Jane now asked for a meeting with the panel, and this time I attended as I had a few questions I wanted answered. They started by saying that with the "head lice" allegation, as they interviewed TTd her story fell apart and it was obvious that she had rehearsed it. With TT's allegation that story also kept changing as well. Then Jane demanded that a full written report should be given to her and one to be kept with her records. The response was amazing with "Why do you want it?" and Jane explained that if ever someone made any accusation whether at St John or at her work, she would have documentary proof of the result. This was especially important as the father was spreading rumours during this time.

Then it was my turn. I asked why Jane was not informed officially about the charge, let alone that there were two allegations. I asked why was no-one allowed to support her during the interview and I asked why the two cadets at the centre of the allegations had not been interviewed. This caused the panel to leave the room and returning five minutes later, they said that they were not at liberty to answer the questions. I then demanded an answer again, to which they refused, so I said "Basically you cocked-up." This was answered with silence.

Why didn't we leave, you may ask, it's simple... we enjoy St John, the learning, treating casualties and teaching, so why should we? Just because of the stupidity of our leaders? It was years later that I learnt that it is illegal to refuse to allow a representative at an inquiry, let alone not to know what the charges are beforehand; hindsight again.

After all this, we went on holiday in the Med for a fortnight and boy if ever a holiday was needed this one was. Some people wonder why I have a reputation of not suffering fools and idiots gladly and questioning our leaders; you can now see why after what we went through and they seem to forget that without us, the members, St John Ambulance would not exist.

Finally at the end of the year I stood down, relinquishing my role and rank and returned to Division as a member, handing over the Division to Sam. My last job in charge was to chase County about Annette's recognition and upon receiving a denial of not knowing anything about it, I rang a contact at NHQ, an old friend, and asked what one had to do to get some action? He checked and came back with the reply that they had not heard anything about it and would I submit it to him, which I did. The following July (2003) Annette was awarded a Meritorious Award and a Letter of Commendation! Hooray, I finally got a result at long last!

****

I planned to stay away from all meetings for three months so that Sam could establish herself as being "in charge" but although this worked out, returning as a first aider did not -- yet another opening for me.

On the 15th of January I was asked if I would take on the role of County Public Relation Officer (CPRO) and also Editor–in-Chief of the Surrey News, with the remit of increasing the public awareness of our activities in the local community. In all my years in St John I would never have thought I would end up being part of County Staff, but as was pointed out to me, Weybridge was the best Division in Surrey at getting press coverage. My aim had always been to get Weybridge in the local papers at least once a month. Looking at the press coverage stats for Surrey, I was amazed to see that although we had thirty nine mentions in the press in 2002, thirteen had come from my Division and another twelve from Hersham; the remaining fourteen were spread between the remaining nineteen Divisions -- not good.

I should have known that my Division would not let me go quietly, a few even had a score to settle, especially Siggie (Jane Signorelli) and a presentation evening was set up in the form of "This is Your Life" complete with the red book, and at the request of my darling daughter, my mother had supplied pictures of me at the age of six months, when I first wore my cadet uniform and the first time I had an adult uniform. Jane even organised for the babysitter to be late so that everyone would be there. I thought that I was going to a lecture until I walked into the HQ. What an evening, with lots of friend from London District as well as Division and Surrey, a Powerpoint presentation with pictures of me when I was young and with dark hair, and some very funny comments. The night finished with me being presented with an engraved decanter.

In April, Joshua was born, on Easter Sunday in fact, weighing in at ten pounds four ounces, so life became hectic again. July saw the whole family attending Clerkenwell to watch me receive my Commander of the Order insignia. For a short time I even became Deputy Commissioner, lasting all of three months. With a young family, two aged parents with serious health problems and to be quite honest, sitting at meetings listening to certain people who only seem to want to build their own empire, was not why I joined St John so I used the "family card" and stood down. I carried on with the PR role though, and by the end of my first year, St John had appeared in the local papers one hundred and eight times with over fifty pictures attached; not a bad result in a year.

2004 started with some bad news. Although I was on County Staff I still attended and went out on duty with Weybridge. In March, a pre-MOT inspection of our Mobile Unit gave us the news that now at the ripe old age of thirty two she was suffering terminal rust and it would not be viable to repair her, as the estimated cost was £18K. Bye bye old girl!

Now the Division began looking for a replacement Mobile Unit, and thinking about how to fund it. I spent the year promoting St John in the media from newspaper articles and taking photographs at events, to live interviews on local radio stations and attending meetings in London at NHQ. This was quite an experience for me; meeting other CPRO's from across England and people from the PR dept. I was the only unpaid volunteer; all the others were paid PR people for the commercial services and NHQ could not understand why I did it, bless them. I could not understand how anyone could be involved in PR for St John without being part of it.

Still the best thing for me in 2004 was after eight years of living together and now with two children, Jane and I got married on her fortieth birthday in August. Sadly, returning from our honeymoon with the boys, my mother who seemed to have waited for us to get married, now happy, passed away three weeks later on November 6th.

2005 followed with the same format of press releases, radio interviews, more meetings at NHQ etc, though we managed to pull a wonderful April fools joke when as editor of the Surrey News, I was asked by Paul Swift, a Weybridge member, if he could place a picture of a helicopter in St John livery, call sign MD902 with Weybridge Division's name on it. Well I could not resist it and a full picture appeared on the back page. Everyone fell for it, even Surrey Ambulance rang up wanting to know who would fly it and where

Another first for Surrey!
Weybridge Division reaches new heights with its most ambitious project ever

April 1st 2005

would it operate from. Well as our commissioner was an army helicopter pilot and Fairoaks aerodrome was not far away from Weybridge it was very easy to sound plausible. Paul even carried on with the gag when shortly after publication on a large duty when he broadcasted on the air, "If you look to the north you should soon see MD 902 flying in." After a short time "Sorry, the cloud has kept MD902 away today".

By the later part of the year I started to become more disillusioned with my role as County PRO. It had started in 2004 when a colleague from Windle Valley Division rang me up asking if I would be at the official opening of their new HQ by the Princess Royal. That was the first I knew about it. County HQ did not seem to think I should be informed.

When I had first taken over the PR dept, I found that County had employed a marketing company to promote St John and paid them £6,000 a year; half being paid by Commercial Services the other by us. I must admit that I assumed that the Commercial Services were getting all the results because we were not, but then speaking to them, I found that they thought we were because *they* were not. I started to put pressure on the marketing company and then we started to get some involvement from them, with them even producing the Surrey News. I think the trouble was that no-one had ever told them what was required from them -- communication!

Suddenly in December I was told that Surrey was stopping using this company as they had a new person to do the job. In fact, Commercial Services only found out when the company rang them and asked what was going on -- communications again.

In January 2006, after many attempts to contact this new person, I finally got to meet her at Weybridge HQ, as I thought at least she could see what we were all about as she had never been in St John, and also Weybridge had taken delivery of their new Mobile First Aid unit; all £140,000 of it. The meeting did not go well. I had the distinct feeling that she was not interested in knowing me, what my role was or what I did, and she referred to the unit as "the county bus," which was not a good start. Then she started to tell me all about the "Breath of Life "campaign that was occurring later on in the year, dates locations etc. All this was news to me; yet again a lack of communication.

Then came the final straw. There were rumours that the members of the NHS Ambulance Service in the Midlands were going on strike. I received an e-mail from NHQ informing us that St John had been advised from the NHS that an industrial dispute would start shortly and St John would be supplying ambulances and crews to work on shifts twenty four hours a day, seven days a week during the strike. I was unaware of this but it turned out that NHQ had signed up to this a few years before. I have no problem with responding to major incidents, as we had done with the bombings in London, air crashes and train crashes etc, but strike breaking?

Within thirty minutes I received another e-mail, this time from the PR dept at NHQ telling all CPRO's not to speak to the press about this as it was confidential; this was after the first e-mail -- a bit late really. Then I had a phone call from one of my friends telling me to look at the "Big White Taxi Service" web site, a clandestine site run by some national ambulance personnel. There it was in bold letters "F****** St John, Strike Breaking" -- this was within a hour of the first release.

Then an e-mail came from our Commissioner informing us that he'd had a request for ambulances and crews to go to the Midlands, and Surrey would be paying £8 an hour to those that volunteered and he would need to take Divisions' vehicles. I was appalled with the e-mail and rang County HQ straight away, pointing out that you couldn't be a volunteer if you were being paid, and what had happened to the "local duties must come first" edict. Within half an hour a fresh e-mail was received. Now members were not going to receive payment but their Divisions would receive money for the use of their equipment and for members' time.

Divisions with members who were health workers in them were up in arms, Superintendents were threatening to take their vehicles off the road to stop them being used, asking about all the local duties they were contracted to cover. It was a shambles, all because certain people wanted to play with ambulances. On top of this, just to compound the problem, the person who was organising all this at NHQ was unfortunately killed in a road accident that weekend.

After speaking to County staff about the strike, the lack of communications etc, I realised I was wasting my time with them. They were not interested in PR; it was not important in their view. I had lost the PR vehicle that we used to promote St John around the county and could not get funding for a new one, yet County HQ bought two new estate cars done up with all the bits for certain people to drive around the County looking cool.

I wrote a letter of resignation with a suggestion that certain people should go on a course and learn how to talk to volunteers and stop being wannabes. I even had it printed in the Surrey News though slightly toned down, but this time I was not going to use the family excuse.

So it was back to Division as an ambulance man, or so I thought. By this time Jane, my wife, had become Superintendent of the Cadet Division and was doing such a good job that she had twenty four cadets and needed help with training and another adult to be there. So guess what? Yes -- I was back where I started -- not as a cadet, but working with the cadets.

After being with them for six months I was asked to apply to be her Divisional Officer, which I did and in March 2007 had to sit in front of a promotion panel. Guess who was on it? Yes, the Commissioner. I could not help smiling to myself as I walked into the room as one of the panel of three was wearing his rank slides the wrong way round. Well I could not resist it as the Commissioner was a stickler for wearing one's medals and insignia correctly, so I asked before we started if there was an initiative test on observation, they all looked very puzzled and said no. I then told the Commissioner how surprised I was that he would have someone on the panel improperly dressed. They still did not get it. I then asked the person if he'd been in Australia or had his wife put on his rank slides that morning, finally the penny dropped and I think that they saw the funny side of it.

It's a great feeling when being interviewed when you don't care whether you get the position or not, and even better when you feel that you have the advantage over them. I had the interview and at the end of it the Commissioner asked if I had anything to ask or say. I looked him in the eye while I considered whether I should say what was on my mind, then I thought, "why not?" Slowly I told them that I would never forgive County for what they put Jane through, not allowing her representation at the Inquiry Board, not being told what the full charges were until the day, treating the two allegations separately and not following the correct protocols. I had waited a long time to be able to air my views and it felt great. Even more so when one of the panel tried to tell me that I was correct and it was law that you are allowed someone at an inquiry and you must be informed what the charges are. I just referred him to the Commissioner to explain why this had not been the case.

Two months later I was confirmed as Jane's Divisional Officer. By now we had twenty cadets attending every Tuesday and with a waiting list of ten more. We decided to start another training evening on a Thursday, and by the time it started in September we had eighteen new members. Jane was keen on the Division entering the County Competitions and for the second year entered a team in the care section. It was their first time in competitions and they came second -- not bad for their first attempt, and they went through to the regional rounds, coming fourth.

When I had returned back to Weybridge, I spoke to Sam about press and we decided to aim at getting an article in one of the local papers at least once a month, and though I was no longer CPRO, I still received e-mails from the PR dept at NHQ. In May I saw that they were looking for a family who were in St John and would be willing to appear on TV. Well at first I did not bother to reply, but then when speaking the PR dept two weeks later I asked if they had any replies I was told no, and they might lose the chance or have to pass it on to the Red Cross. Well I couldn't let that happen, so I offered up myself as a candidate. They then asked me if I had been to any major events like Princess Diana's funeral and whether any of my family was also involved with St John. Bless them -- by the time I had finished they said I sounded like the right person for the job and would get the TV Company to contact me.

I was rung by the producer of the GMTV morning programme the following day, who wanted to know my background and get some photographs. She asked me if I knew what it was all about, which I had to admit I didn't. It turned out that Mr John Nichol, (a former RAF fighter pilot who had been shot down, captured and tortured before being paraded on their television during the first Gulf War) had put forward an idea about a programme on the everyday heroes who gave their time free and were hardly ever recognised.

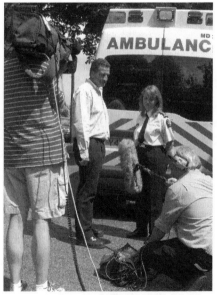

The other organisations to appear were going to be the Royal National Life Boat Institution, Rapid Response, Mountain Rescue Service & First Response and the idea was for John Nichol to spend a day with each, filming and then broadcasting them on the morning programme -- one a day for a week. Then came the tricky bit -- how to get everyone together on a duty they could film at. In the end it could not have worked out better. Dorking Division was covering a half marathon at Bookham. We filmed in the morning on a lovely day with the backdrop of a Surrey village, then it was onto Weybridge HQ to film an interview with my wife and then my daughter Sam. Then they wanted to go onto the Regatta that we were covering that day and film Alex, my grandson putting a sling on John, while talking to him. We had started filming at nine in the morning and finished at four; all that time for just five minutes of fame on GMTV, although they did show it twice in the morning.

As they say everyone has three minutes of fame in their lifetime; ours was a bit longer. Of course, I could not let this happen without getting it into the local press, and this was the beginning of a run of press releases that you could not have planned if you tried.

It started with one of our cadets, Henry Baines, who was nearly seventeen. While on holiday in France, in July, he saved a young Italian life, and then in August was involved with other members from another Division in saving a man's life who suffered a heart attack. Then in September, he attended a road traffic accident and was complemented by the Ambulance service. This meant, without planning, we appeared in the local papers each week continually for three months, August to October due to the papers having different days for deadlines.

In November, we had the Annual Inspection of the Cadets so again we appeared in the local papers. I said to Sam that I thought that we had our fair share of press this year so I would lay off now 'til next year.

How wrong can one be, as in the beginning of December we made the headlines big time! With hindsight I suppose I should have seen it coming! After the boat being damaged in the gales, and then the mobile unit being hit by a tent in the great gale, me getting hypothermia on duty, the near miss with the lightning at Brooklands; it was getting closer and finally the elements caught up with me. On this particular Sunday morning four of us were on duty as usual at Esher Rugby Club. It was very windy with heavy rain squalls coming in.

At the club there was a long line of eighty foot high poplar trees at the back of the stand, so being sensible I parked the ambulance windward of them so that we were safe, or so I thought. About midday a casualty came on board with a ankle injury, and as it was my son-in-law we were all in the back taking the mickey out of him when the wind started to roar and turned around a hundred and eighty degrees.

The next thing I knew was there was an almighty crash and one of the rear windows shattered as a branch of a tree came through it and the roof fell in on top of us. One of the trees snapped of at the base crushing a car next to it and the rest coming down on top of us. It all went very quiet for a couple of seconds. Then I said "SHIT! We are supposed to be on duty this afternoon." Exiting the ambulance very quickly, we were amazed to see this tree lying on top of it.

A quick check revealed that no-one appeared to be injured and the ambulance had possibly saved the under 12's from injury as they were just walking past the front of the vehicle when the tree came down.

My next action was to ring Sam to let her know what had happened, then Jane as we had a cadet with us. She came over straight away, followed by BBC Southern Counties Radio who passed me straight through to do a live broadcast there and then. One of the guys retrieved my camera from the cab, so I took lots of pictures; well it's not often you see an ambulance with a tree on it. My mobile then started to ring with BBC radio wanting to know if there were any photos of it and asking when they could have them. This was followed by the BBC TV news who also wanted pictures of the incident.

Ringing the AA was fun explaining that we had a tree on top of us, and as for filling the accident claim form, well I've been here before. We appeared on the BBC website and BBC TV London News at six thirty and ten p.m.; the story run in the local papers right up to Christmas. The next day I had a very terse e-mail from NHQ asking why I had not notified them about the incident as they had phone calls from national newspapers about it that morning and knew nothing about it. I explained to them that as it happened on Sunday lunchtime I had rung NHQ and only got an answerphone and on Monday morning with two young children to get to school, suffering from cancer and having to go for treatment every morning the only word I could think to say to them had two "L"s in it.

The story appeared again in the local papers in late January when the trees were cut down and some people were up in arms about where the hundreds of green parrots that roosted there would go. As it was the third tree that had fallen down in the last four years and the club had them inspected only three months prior to our incident, they had to go.

Amazingly, they repaired the ambulance at a cost of £24,000 though it took nearly a year before it was returned back to us; in fact it came back the same week as our new replacement, in November 2008.

During this time Cobham Division loaned us their ambulance for the first four months of 2008 as they had no duties for it, then County loaned us a old vehicle that was available which saw us through the summer season. Compared to our modern crusaders it felt like one could hold a barn dance inside it with so much space. It was nice to get a new vehicle eventually, apart from the fact that it had to be returned back to Cambridge straight away to have lots of minor faults corrected.

2008 turned out to be a good year for the Cadet Division. One of our Cadets, Sam Smedley, attended a road traffic incident and organised getting an ambulance as well as someone to get a first aid kit from a shop  and dealing with the casualty, all this at the age of twelve; for this Sam received a Commanders Commendation.

This year we entered two teams in the County Care competitions; they came first and third; the first team losing winning at the Regional round by just one point. In October, at the annual Transfer of the County Colour, the flag (the Colour) dedicated in memory of past members of Surrey St John, held by a Division for a year is then transferred to another Division. In days past, this meant from East Surrey to West Surrey but with the numbers of Divisions reduced this no longer applies. The event is held in a church where awards are presented. This year it was Weybridge's turn to receive the Colour and it was decided to make up the colour party of two Badgers *[5-10 yr olds]*, two Cadets and one adult who would carry it; a first in the county. Also Weybridge Cadet Henry Baines received the Alex Clarke award for the Cadet with the highest number of public duty hours in the past year; an impressive three hundred and thirty five hours.

In the summer we attended a three-day open air concert held at Mercedes-Benz World at Brooklands. Friday and Sunday was Sir Elton John, and on the Saturday it was the Sugababes and McFly. I saw Sir Elton back in the seventies at Earls Court, then to see him thirty five years later, he still had it. Both his nights were a sell out, though the night I went to, the Friday, it poured down and it resembled a mini Glastonbury, mud and all; still I would not have missed it for the world.

2009 saw a possible new era in the history of the Pennocks in St John, with Jamie, on reaching his tenth birthday, joining Weybridge cadets. Who knows?

In all the years I've been in St John I have been in the air, on the water, seen the inside of Buckingham Place, and attended many great stage shows in London. Locally, I have seen all the major pop groups as well as great artists, and treated so many injured people that I could not even imagine how many. I have resuscitated ten people, and met my second wife and would not change it at all. It's a wonderful way to meet people, to socialise and give back something to the local community. What better then to help someone who's injured, be the Good Samaritan, and do it as a volunteer just for the love of it.

I have seen lots of changes, some good, some not so good and some down right daft. Unfortunately the vast number of people now at National Headquarters have never been in St John and do not understand how volunteers work, feel or why they do what they do for no pay.

I have seen so many changes of uniforms and even now we are changing because someone says we need to modernise our image yet again -- will this bring in new members? I doubt it. It did not in the past, and all it will do is cost the Divisions more money which they can ill afford.

In the seventies, eighties and early nineties there were no risk assessments or health and safety, no need for certificates for this and that before we are allowed to save lives. If there had been, would we been allowed to do the demos, pop concerts and Notting Hill Carnival etc? I doubt it - too dangerous! If only we were not ruled by lawyers and accountants with the "but what if" mentality.

I joined to do first aid and that is what I still do, in the pouring rain, howling wind in the middle of a rugby pitch on a cold winter's day or at a fete on a hot summer's day. It is one of the best feelings in the world to be able to help someone that's injured.

APPENDIX 1

MEMORIES OF BEXHILL CAMP

I heard about the National Camp at Bexhill from our Area Commissioner Mary Douglas, who had been praising it's virtues for some time, (she used to take her Division Ash Vale there), and now she went there for the whole six weeks of summer working with the Camp Commandant, Miss Win Willis.

In 1979, for the first of many visits to camp we took seven Cadets plus our two, who were in the junior section, not knowing what to expect. We had visions that we might be digging our own latrines and washing in a stream as well as eating outside after catching it, but Mary had assured us it was not anything like that and was very civilised. She was right; first there was a toilet block with a shower unit for both boys and girls with hot water, a large recreation hall, and then a fully equipped first aid room to deal with any problems, a dining hall that could house over a hundred and fifty hungry cadets in one sitting and a well equipped kitchen with a full time cook. The tents were the old style white army bell tents and were Divided into three units, the boys at one end of the field, the adults in the middle and the girls at the other end.

We had managed to borrow the Scouts' mini bus from my brother-in-law to transport everyone down to the camp and with taking our car we just had enough space for the Cadets and all our baggage. The old Transit mini bus had seen better days and it was well before all the regulations that are now are in force.

The Cadets called it "the Red Can'ardly" as it could hardly climb some of the hills on the way to camp.

Mind you, it was probably overloaded. About the third year of use, I noticed the floor on the driver's side seemed a bit spongy and when I lifted up the floor carpet I could see though to the road where the floor had rotted away.

The camp was just outside Bexhill in a small village called Sidley, which consisted of a bank, a fish and chip shop and a general store -- and of course, a pub. On arrival, after four thirty, so that the camp staff could clear up from the previous week and get prepared for us, we had a cuppa and a sticky bun. If we were lucky we would be allocated a tent that had already been put up; in all the

years we went there this never happened, so we had the joy of pitching our own tent which would need at least six people to do it.

This is where the St John and the camping spirit kicked in with nearly everyone helping everybody. There was one odd Division one year that did not take part in anything for some unknown reason, but with the rest you soon got to know people. There were Divisions from Nettleham in Lincolnshire, Maidstone in Kent, Shirley, Penge and other Divisions from London as well as Hazlegrove from Manchester, Tamworth from Staffordshire and Bagshot and Ash Vale from Surrey to name just a few.

Friendships were soon made that have stood the passage of time. I still see Trevor and Joan Constable who ran Shirley at the Surrey Dinner Dance even now. Once we were all settled in, and after dinner, there was a meeting for everyone to run through the Do's and Don'ts of the camp. This was followed by an Officers and adults meeting to work out who did what and when for the week. Each day a Division or Divisions took it in turns to be in charge of the camp for a day starting at eight o'clock in the evening for twenty four hours. During the day, that Division had to do the tent inspections, have the toilets and showers cleaned and stocked, empty all the rubbish bins around the site, peel the spuds for the evening meal, clear away and tidy up the eating hall after each sitting, help serve and wash up in the kitchen.

Also proficiency subjects had to be taught, the standard ones being camp craft, map reading, (this involved a mini hike for the younger ones and a midnight hike for the older ones), nature study for the Juniors, and as I worked in the motor trade I taught the motorist subject; later on I would take my make-up kit and teach casualty simulation for a change

On Sunday, we went straight after breakfast to change into uniform to go to the Church Service held in the  recreation hall, and who can ever forget "Kum Bah Ya" played on a guitar by the cleric's daughter every year? We have tried! The routine for the rest of the week was well established. Breakfast was served at eight o' clock prompt. At nine forty five prompt, the St John flag was raised on the flagpole as everyone stood in a square around it. This was followed by the morning prayer with any notices for the day being given out, and it was decided whether the brailing (part of the tent) was to be tied up or not. Then it was on to finishing laying out their bedding and uniform, face flannels, tooth brushes etc; for inspection. Tents received extra marks for making gadgets, usually from wood and string, the wood coming from the woods next to the camp site. At the end of the week, the tent with the most number of points won the Best Kent Tent Award. Also, it was a sneaky way of checking if the Cadets had washed their faces and cleaned their teeth, and it also aired the tent. After this, at ten fifteen, the tuck shop opened, after that the Cadets went to their proficiency subjects, working till twelve then at twelve thirty it was lunch after which it was their free time.

For those of us with transport, we had trips for at least four afternoons. The favourite was going to Hastings, but we had trips to Bodiam Castle, Battle Abbey and the sea at Bexhill or Eastbourne. If you stayed on camp, games were organised to keep you entertained the favourite being "It's a Knockout". Evening supper was at six thirty.

The evening time was quite hectic as entertainment was organised from seven thirty onwards. This would include a Topsy Turvy evening were the boys dressed as girls and visa versa, a "Talent Contest" on another, five-a-side football matches or rounder's on another, and the midnight hike for the map reading group followed the Thursday bonfire with the cadets sitting around it singing songs and eating chips.

The Duty Officer would be sent to the local chip shop to collect more than a hundred and fifty plus portions; still at least we would ring the order through to give them a chance. The evenings always ended with camp cocoa and biccies being served between half nine and ten before retiring to bed. Lights out was by ten thirty.

On Friday, there was always the "Goodbye Disco" and the presentations of certificates for the week by Miss Willis. The following morning would be taken up with packing and sad and sometimes tearful goodbyes before the trip back home.

On the way back we (Weybridge) always stopped at a Happy Eater for a midday lunch, which Kate and I paid for ourselves, and after leaving there, within ten minutes all the cadets were fast asleep and only woke up when we got back to Weybridge HQ.

Arriving home our house seemed huge after living in a small tent and the joy of being in a normal bed after lying on a Lillo all week! The downside was the piles of washing, but we went to camp for a total of nine years, and we would not have gone each year if we had not enjoyed it so much.

It was not all work though. Over the years we all got up to silly antics, both the Cadets and us Officers. One morning during flag, a van drove up and out jumped four masked people dressed in black, who snatched the duty officer, and leaving a ransom note, drove out of camp.

Another time, as luck would have it, we had visitors from NHQ. Someone had switched the flag and as it was broken open it was not ours but a Red Cross flag. NHQ officers did not know whether to 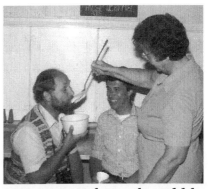 salute or not. It was quite common to have the odd bra and knickers float down as the flag unfolded. On another occasion as we assembled together by the flagpole was a hospital bed with a body in it covered up with a blanket. Miss Willis walked around it and as there was no sign of movement she, probably thinking it was a Resusci-Anne, went to pull the blanket off. D/S Geoff Nice from Lincolnshire sat up and said "Boo!" Poor Miss Willis -- did she jump, and trying to keep a straight face, tried to tell him off in front of us all; then she got into the bed with him.

Win Willis was a wonderful person; God bless her soul. She had a great sense of humour and tolerated lots of pranks but knew when it went too far, and could be a good disciplinarian when it was needed. She told us during the first year that we went to camp, that she had a visit from someone at National HQ, a retired army "bod" who said she needed an assault course built for the cadets to train on.

This was typical of people who have no idea of what St John is all about and although she objected to it on safety grounds and the age span of the Cadets, she was overruled and it was built by the army the following year when the camp was not in use. Well, by the time we arrived at camp it had been opened for two weeks. The pits that had been dug and had sand put into them were now full of muddy water. Already in the two weeks there had been numerous injuries, and Win had stopped the use of it when a cadet broke their leg. By the following year National HQ had contractors come in to dismantle it and fill in the pits.

One morning, as we walked into the hall for breakfast, there were no tables or benches. Then someone pointed out they were on the roof; the whole lot of them. As I cannot stand heights, it wasn't me who put them there! Once while out driving, I noticed a bus stop that had been knocked down in a road accident not far from the camp. So Geoff, Paul Roots (a Weybridge member), Del boy and a couple of others carried it into the camp early one morning and propped it up by the dinner hall. Paul then demanded tickets from the cadets before letting them in for breakfast. Again we got told off by Win, with a twinkle in her eye and had to return it back to where we got it from.

Shirley Division Cadets pulled a memorable prank; they had acquired a police "road shut Diversion" sign and placed it at the entrance of the camp on a Saturday afternoon. Of course all the Divisions turning up followed the Diversion arrow into Sidley. Well there is no other entrance to the camp, and by five o'clock, Win was beginning to get worried as nobody had turned up except Shirley Division. Then she received phone calls from lost people and she then rumbled what was going on. Good old Win -- she played along with the prank by saying nothing, but the following morning at flag said that the local police would be visiting the camp over the stolen sign as it was theft and would want to interview the culprits after Church Service; her timing was impeccable.

Win had her favourites from the Leaders with Trevor and Roger from Shirley Division, Geoff and I at the top of the list. Geoff was one of the main instigators of some of the pranks. It was him that brought a tape recording of the sound of stampeding cattle which was played through the flap of tents in the early mornings. It was Geoff who with us would turn a tent round ninety degrees while the occupants were asleep, so when they woke up the entrance was in the wrong place. This worked very well when we had a contingent from the Order of Malta from Ireland. It was Geoff who after being kept awake by one of the adult members talking 'til all hours, got up early one morning at six and played reveille on a bugle into the guy's tent.

We all did a runner so he had no idea who had done it, but he was furious and his mood was not helped when he came into breakfast to find the bugle hanging from the roof over his table. He went to see Win clutching the bugle but before he could say anything she said "Ah, I see you have my bugle, thank you for returning it."

Geoff used to tell Win the only reason he kept coming to camp was her camp custard, so one evening after the main meal she presented him with a huge, and I mean huge, bowl of custard. Geoff, not to be out done ate the lot? The following evening, we changed over the chocolate sauce for Daddies brown sauce. He poured it over his custard and we waited for his reaction; he ate the lot. He did say later on that it tasted terrible but he was not going to let anybody know. On his final day at camp that year, at Flag and while standing to attention, out walked Miss Willis and, as it turned out many years later my future son in law, a cadet from Shirley. In his hand, behind his back a custard pie, which was pushed into Geoff's face. He just wiped it from his face and ate it.

Our worst experience at camp happened one Tuesday afternoon on our duty day; with only Paul and Kathy

Roots, and Kate and I on camp and seeing a boy standing by the girls' toilets I went to find out what was going on. He explained that his sister was inside with a problem, so calling over Kate and Kathy they went in to find a young girl trying to scrub her hair with a scrubbing brush. On inspection the girl who had long hair and I thought was blond/grey was in fact teaming with head lice. None of us had ever seen anything like it before. Paul and I were sent down to Sidley to get nit combs and bottles of special hair shampoo. We spent all afternoon washing and combing the girl's hair. When Win and Mary came back from shopping for the camp they were amazed at what we had found. In fact Mary would not believe it until one of the lice jumped of the girl's hair onto her shoulder. It turned out the girl had been sent to camp with this problem and had been suffering from them for weeks, and though we asked if we could cut the girls hair, her Superintendent refused to let us. All the other cadets in the tent were found to be infected as was the whole of the bedding and even the tent. That night, having spent all afternoon with head lice and their eggs, what was for dinner – RICE!   No thanks -- we all went out for a meal. The following year the girl turned up at camp with short hair.

There are so many stories that can be told about camp, it would fill a book, but it was a wonderful place. It taught the cadets to care for themselves, to share and work together as a team, learn to give and take (most of the time), and strengthen the loyalty and the feeling of belonging to their own Division.

APPENDIX 2

MEMORIES OF TRAINING FOR LONDON DISTRICT

Having been offered a position as a casual trainer at York Street, I, with foreboding, started there in November 1986, and to be honest did not think I was capable of standing up in front of twenty people and teaching them. Let's be fair -- I'm dyslexic and don't speak as posh as the other instructors. Also, they had been doing it a long time. But Iris Bundle and the other trainers were so supportive and helpful. Iris said to me one day "Give it three months and I bet you that you will not want to give it up." She was right. Oscar Wilde once said "The best job in the world is to teach your hobby." I loved it, though I still was not confident in myself. The job was an odd one insofar as it was not full time, you got no sick pay or holiday entitlement and if there was no work you did not get paid, but you still paid tax and National Insurance.

London District HQ on York Street was also a training centre. The second floor consisted of two large classrooms that could hold up to twenty four students each. The ground floor was where the training admin was and the basement was where all the equipment for all the training centres around London was kept. As it had car parking spaces I would drive there. It was before the days of congestion charges, and believe it or not, in all the time I worked there, I never came across a road traffic incident, although I did stop at a car that was on fire once.

The training team at York Street consisted of Ann Cable, who is now (2008) London District Commissioner, John Newman who went on to work from National HQ, Eff Orwell who was a teacher from the East End who had been attacked and beaten up quite badly, but was a smashing woman with an infectious laugh and a lovely smile. There was also John Blatch, an ex-policeman, and Gerry, but I cannot remember his other name, who was a mature gentleman. There were others but they were mainly working at the other centres and occasionally came into York Street. I nicknamed Ann "the ice lady," because she was so professional but did not laugh, and talked to her students as a school teacher would, whereas I liked to interact with them, but at this time it was not the done thing. I even got told off because there was too much laughter in my class, but I found out that my students seemed to enjoy the course more if it was fun.

One day, while lying down on the floor as a "casualty" for the initial assessment for Ann I could not resist blowing into her ear as she checked for my breathing. She just collapsed on top of me laughing fit to bust; she even chased me out of the class. From then on, teaching became fun with her and I began to settle into the job and would stay working for them for the next ten years of my life.

One day it dawned on me that as Iris had once said to me when I first started -- I had a wealth of experience with all my years in St John, and while teaching a class one day, I thought these students had come here to learn because they did not know what to do in a first aid situation. I did. I had resuscitated people, treated severe bleeding and fractures, seen heart attacks, strokes, drug overdoses and stabbings -- my students had not, and suddenly the confidence was there. I stopped trying to be something I wasn't and became myself.

I was then sent out to other training centres and worked at Kingston, Feltham, Ealing and Croydon, as well as being sent to companies to teach. One of the most horrendous places was Camden Council. I was told to dress down and wear jeans and a jumper, and was not allowed to call a whiteboard "white" -- it was a neutral board, and when I held a door open for a woman who was carrying a package she turned to me and said, "That's a sexist action." I just said "Stuff you" and walked off; this was political correctness (PC) gone mad. I was having lunch with some of the students and I asked them their feelings. One guy said he didn't think his colour was an issue until he worked there and now some of his work colleagues were frightened to talk to him in case they said something wrong and got the sack.

When I returned to York Street, I asked never to be sent there again, although I then used to start my courses with "I don't care whether you're male, female, straight, gay, black, coloured or white -- we all bleed the same way, and

I cannot do this PC stuff. If I upset you please tell me and I will apologise to you in front of the class," and though my other fellow trainers were horrified, none of my students ever complained.

In the early years I was sent to venues in South East London. One was an art college, and when I was demonstrating the recovery position on one of the students, as I placed his arm outwards I saw that he had a gun in a holster under his arm pit. The other time was also another college, and as I patted him down before rolling him over I felt a large knife on him. Even while teaching, I still had people to treat in my class, lots of faints, a few seizures, but one or two more serious ones too. On one occasion, a student collapsed and stopped breathing, I was giving him CPR when I realised that the rest of the class were just sitting watching me, they thought It was part of the course, and it was only when I swore at them and told them to call a ambulance that they realised it was for real. Another time, a lady collapsed unconscious, was breathing, but her face kept changing colour from pale to flushed and then back to pale. Her pulse was fast, then slow and then irregular, then back to fast. After placing her in recovery position, we dialled 999. I learnt later that she was having a stroke and a heart attack at the same time, but my class gave me 10 out of 10 for the recovery position.

I also learned early in my teaching career that assumption can make an ass of you. At the end of one particular day, I turned round to a very good looking young lady and said "You can go home and practice what you have learned on your boyfriend tonight," as I noticed she was not wearing a wedding ring. In a loud voice, she said "It's not my boyfriend, it's my girlfriend." From that day on, I always used the word partner. I also learned to look at people's faces and eyes and found that I could very quickly assess their mood.

West Indian students were great and often I could have a laugh with them. Once on a course, we had a Rastafarian with long dreadlocks and as he checked Annie to see if she was breathing, I got the giggles as I could not see which way he was looking and it looked like she had a cat sitting on her head. At this a big smiling face looked up at me and said "Trouble with you white honkies is you don't understand our religion." I just said I wasn't worried about that but could he give me a clue to which way was he looking. We both burst out laughing, as did the rest of the class. At tea break, I got him to tell me all about the Rastafarian religion as it is always useful to know about other things.

A couple of years later, Del boy had become a trainer and he and another trainer were given the job of going to Notting Hill to teach the Carnival stewards some basic first aid and to work. Both Del and I got rid of our ties and jackets that we normally wore to give a relaxed atmosphere but the other trainer was insistent that we would keep them on. Then he had an opening remark of "Now all you lot..." At this remark, I could see them reacting, so I grabbed him and took him outside to explain the facts of life, and if he didn't want to get knifed he had to be quiet. After that, the course went OK until we asked for them to practice resus on the dolls. You can imagine the comments about a white doll, but no-one would volunteer until I picked on one of the steward's sons aged about 10, to have a go. He did it perfectly and I then asked him what he thought as none of the adults would try, his comment was, "They're a load of w******." At this one of the biggest guys in the class stood up, complete with all the gold chains and rings, (he looked like Mr T) and said no one called him that, and then got down and did resus. Once that had happened they all tried it.

London District seemed only interested in teaching First Aid at Work courses and if anyone requested anything out of the ordinary or to be taught at odd times, they would ask one of us if we were interested. Well I was, and started too build up reputations for teaching these courses. They included courses for ski instructors, tour operator reps, groups going abroad on expeditions in either the jungle or the desert etc; and because of the accounts system in London, it was left to me to charge for my services and keep the money. The Davies group of wine bars was one of these clients, passed to me by York Street. They wanted a course run over two evenings at the main bar in Tooley Street, next to the London Dungeon from seven to ten p.m. This led to me doing this for the next four years and even going to Exeter for two days in 1997 teaching their people. Another job was to contact a woman who wanted a course for her group of masseurs on Saturdays. Anya, a Dutch lady, ran a school that needed the students to do a basic first aid course and this turned into a regular event twice a year 'til 2004.

One job York Street gave me in December 1992 was at Simply Ski, a company that took skiers by train to the Alps for skiing holidays. The first two courses were held at their head office in Chiswick, and involved teaching first aid on the ski slopes and at the chalets that the skiers stayed in. In 1994 they asked me if I would mind going out to the Alps in December to teach it. Well I jumped at the chance. I flew to Lyon airport where I was picked up and had a one and a half hour drive to Meribel for the first two years, then Courcheval for the third year. The first year there was no snow yet and the scenery was beautiful with just the mountain tops covered.

The second year at Lyon saw me getting some action. While waiting to be picked up, I suddenly heard a commotion. A man had fallen over and had quite a serious head wound that was bleeding profusely; unfortunately he was French and drunk, and as I cannot speak a word of French this proved interesting. While I was trying to attend to him, I heard a click and looked up to see a Gendarme with his sub-machine gun pointing at me. I thought saying I was a first aider or St John probably would not work, so I yelled "medic" which seemed to work and then shortly afterwards an ambulance turned up and took over. My lift turned up and presented me with a shovel as there was three foot of snow at the resort and we would have to dig our way into our chalet.

Then on the third day one of the ski instructors fell over in the snow and headbutted a concrete post and yet again there was more blood for me to treat. The final year, again my skills were needed. This time the company had brought over a driving instructor to teach them how to drive on the snow. I had an afternoon off and went with them. Everything was alright until we went up to the 3000 metre level where he developed mountain sickness, and I had to bring him back down to the village.

It seemed that I was one of those people that wherever I went, I came across accidents. I even went to Rhodes with Kate on holiday and a Russian fell over at the airport and broke his leg -- why me? Still I managed to spend three weeks in Australia without treating any one while visiting Neil who was living there.

Back in 1989, Eff had asked me if I wanted to earn some money on the side; this was before I started to pick up the other work. Eff also worked at the University of London teaching first aid and wanted assistance in the practical sessions. Now this was a new experience for me. In St John, we taught a ratio of twelve students to one trainer. At Uni, they would teach the theory in a lecture hall at Senate House with up to sixty students to one lecturer and they would often be a doctor or a professor. I attended one such lesson on blood, it lasted over an hour and a half with so much technical information, I was totally lost and, looking at the students, so were they. As far as I was concerned blood was red and you had to stop it, and who cared how many pints went through the heart in an hour and how the blood was made up etc. Only after the lecture were the student numbers broken down to a twelve to one ratio for the practical sessions. Not only that but they had to sign for a numbered triangle bandage, one each, and I would swap them round so when they handed them back, it mucked up their paperwork. As for the Annies, they were brought out only once for them to practice on then locked away until the day of the assessment. Still, the money was good and regular for a couple of years. Unfortunately the doctor who ran the course, who was a really very nice guy, had not taught his wife any first aid and when he had a heart attack she did not know what to do and he died at home aged only 42.

It's funny how things work out though. Three years later, I was sent to the Uni by York Street to teach a one day course and I met one of the occupational nurses who used to be at Senate House. She said that the Uni was looking for someone to teach their courses who could adapt to the environment that the students worked in.

They had tried St John but they would only teach the basic course. I explained that I could but could not issue certificates, but that did not matter to them as they were registered with the HSE and issued their own. I ended up teaching at the Uni one week in every month for the next ten years, only giving up when I had a health problem; even then returning to do the odd job.

One of the most enjoyable jobs I had to do occurred in February 1993. I was called into the office and asked if would mind teaching a one day course split over four or five days to forty or more students. Well they knew me, always up for a challenge, so then they told me where; Amsterdam. Great! I'd never been there before.

I had to go by train to Harwich, catch the ferry over to the Hook of Holland, then be picked up and driven to the hotel. The company was Kontiki Tours, an Australian based company that took young Aussies and Kiwis on coach tours around Europe, and they wanted me to teach the young reps a sort of first aid course. This involved resus in between the seats of a coach, and drink related injuries etc -- right up my street; also no-one around from York Street to interfere. I love working with Aussies and Kiwis. I had worked with an Aussie for ten years in the motor trade. They will tell you to your face what they think, and they are so friendly. So when I arrived I was taken straight into the bar to meet everyone. They were all half my age but that didn't matter to them. Only four out of the forty four had not done first aid before as they all were taught it in school back home. The four were Brits and the rest could not believe that despite England being surrounded with water, it was not taught at school.

The reps were not only doing first aid, they had to budget and buy food, cook it and present it to the rest of the group. They had to do the finance; not only buying food but filling in accounts to be presented at the end of the week, so each day was quite a full day for them. But they always found time to party in the evening; often I would be dragged out of my bed at eleven at night to go out clubbing. I learned Aussie rule football one night on an open air ice rink. Another time, I learned the Maori Hakka standing on a pedalo boat in the middle of one of the canals in Amsterdam.

We visited Anne Frank's Museum; that was quite a sobering experience, and of course the red light district, where one of the girls said she had bigger boobs then the girl in the window and then flashed them. Then a pimp came out to chat her up, which ended in a slight punch up. I think maybe they took me with them to be their first aider, though my liver would never be the same after the seven days I spent with them.

The journey home to England was fun as they all were returning. They stated drinking at nine in the morning as we left the hotel, arriving at the customs they all, bar two, had to go through the foreigner's part. One had a row with the official as she had a Basotho passport which was a British Protectorate so she was British. Also one of them had undone an Annie case and left just the hand sticking out. We found out that Dutch custom officials do not have a sense of humour, but eventually we all got onto the ferry where they carried on drinking. Back in the UK, on the coach trip to London, still more drink then on to the International Hotel in Russell Square, and into the bar.

When my wife Kate picked me up from there I was in a sorry state. Thank goodness when I got home I found out that the following day's job had been cancelled. I slept all day, but what memories.

With all this extra income I was earning, I went and found an accountant as I was worried about the tax man. Supplying him with all the information, he duly filled in all the papers and submitted them. Both he and I were surprised to receive a letter from them making me self-employed. He actually told me that in all the years he had never known that to happen.

While working at York Street, it was inevitable that I would be in contact with London District officers and I was often called upstairs to their offices to discuss the availability of the Division for this duty or that duty, rather then ring me at home. This annoyed Surrey HQ, but if the request went through Surrey, by the time we received it the duty would be over. This meant that I had a close friendship with them all, which led to us being offered to cover perk events like the London theatres, and events at the Royal Albert Hall as London often struggled to get them covered, and as I was working most of the time in London, I could meet Kate or someone else and go onto the event, bearing in mind the there was no charge for these duties.

I have always believed in fate, having resuscitated a few people and only having two survive. I held on to the thought that if it was their day to die they died. I just tried to give them a chance of life.

In February 1995, I received a call from York Street one Monday morning asking if I could go to Hammersmith the next day and teach a four day course as the trainer booked for this had been injured that morning in an RTC. Now bear in mind I had never been to Hammersmith training centre before -- anyhow I started the course then about nine fifteen received a phone call from York Street. They had two young ladies who had turned up there for a course but the course had started the day before and asked if I'd take them on my course; if so they would bring them over. Funny old world -- these two arrived about nine forty, and as the last one came into the hall I said to her, "It's a bummer when you turn up late, don't worry you have not missed much, have a seat and I will tell you what you missed at tea break."

From this beginning, who would have thought that this beautiful young woman who looked like a model and was so well dressed, (she worked for Jaeger the woman's fashion chain), would end up being the next Mrs Pennock? If the trainer had not been injured, if Jane had not got the days wrong, if York Street had not brought her over to Hammersmith, if, if, if, etc: FATE.

I had always kept away from being attracted to any student, though there was always the opportunity. One of my colleagues was a lad for the girls even though he was married. I could never understand it; he wasn't good looking, but he just seemed to be able to pull 'til one morning he came into York Street looking like someone had hit him in the face with a frying pan. Someone had -- it was his wife.

At the end of this particular course, I went for a drink with them all, which I did not often do as I would have to drive home afterwards. However it had been a good course, apart from when I had asked them all "Who has broken anything?" in the fractures lesson. Well, we had all the usual sports injuries and minor ones, and as I went round the group, Jane answered with a huge list of injuries and I said, "Road accident or just accident prone?" She looked me in the eyes and answered, "No--- child abuse," then went flushed in the face with embarrassment. I just died on my feet, no-one had ever answered with that. Quickly passing on, I went to the next student. At tea break I went up to her to apologise for embarrassing her, and then dropped myself further in it by assuming it was her father that had done it, only to be told, "No it was my mother." At the pub, she said that as she had learned so much she would like to carry on and use the skills that she had acquired and go further with it. I explained about joining St John and found out where she lived; Kenley, in Surrey. I told her to try the local Division but if they looked at her as if she had two heads, or just sat and talked about the last war then she should come to Weybridge as we were a very active unit with a high standard of training. Two months later I received a phone call from Jane and she joined the Division in May.

In the ten years of working at York Street, I had seen many changes. When I first started we used OHP and slides, then came the video with "super John" John Newman as the first aider in it, with a huge manual to go with it. We have been called trainers, instructors and facilitators. We had a change to the recovery position. We all said was that the change was dangerous but were told from National HQ that basically, we did not know what we were talking about. Six months later and a few recorded injuries to students, it was replaced by the original method, though the comment was that although there were no problems with it, it was being changed back for safety reasons.

I had worked with some smashing people; Iris Bundle who was like a big sister to me, Carol Locke who went onto work for National HQ, Sue Warner, Mark McGee, Dave and Yvonne Dormer, Del Boy and Jayne Signorelli who went on to become a Paramedic in America. Jayne still could be fooled into believing that the two clocks by the M4 flyover had different times due to the fact they faced opposite ways and the sun caused the difference. I kept that up for a week before she rumbled me.

After ten years of travelling to York Street, I began thinking that maybe I would be better off working for Surrey, as my HQ was used for courses and was only five miles away from home. I would not have the one and a half hour journey up the M25 and M4 each day and then again back home. Mr Ralph Brown who had started as a trainer at York Street, and who I had worked with, (in fact he still remembered the first job we ever did together, and we knew each other from stock-car racing as he was in charge of Cranleigh Division), was now in charge of Surrey's courses, though the rate of pay was less then London if you took in the time and the fuel price into consideration. Well, it was time for me to change, so in July 1996 I stopped working for York Street, and started working for Surrey but still as a casual trainer, allowing me to carry on doing my other work.

I was now a Royal Yacht Association (RYA) first aid trainer; this came about late in 1983 when Queen Mary's Sailing Club (QMSC) had asked me to teach a one day first aid course to their rescue teams and instructors. No problems with all the experience that I had gained from being on the water for the last seven years. It went down well as it covered drowning, fractures, dislocations and hypothermia -- so well that I got asked to do another one in January, and I did not think there was anything odd about doing one so soon after the first one.

The clubhouse was rather full; but I carried on teaching. It wasn't until I was talking about what to do with the casualty while waiting for an ambulance that someone said that where they were, if the tide was out they could be half a mile from the shore. I thought, tide at this reservoir? I asked the gentleman where he sailed. "Skegness" came the reply. I then went round the whole group and they were from Cornwall to Northumberland as well as some from the club. It turned out that because of the good feedback from the first course, QMSC had advertised this course at the forthcoming boat show in London.

At the end of the day, people came up to me and said how good a course it was. They had been on others where it had been taught by people who had no sailing experience and could not answer questions on what to do in an emergency on the water. Weeks later, I had a phone call from the RYA wanting to know all about the course and its content and by the end of the year it was adopted with a few changes and became the official RYA first aid course.

On one of these courses at QMSC the students got to see an incident first hand. I had just started demonstrating resus when I was called. A sailing boat had capsized and a crewman had been taken down while still attached to the harness. I jumped into a waiting safety boat and eventually with four guys on the centre board the boat eventually came up and we got him into our boat, a RIB. I had never practiced let alone done resus in a RIB before, but we got him to shore and he was one of the lucky ones that survived though he was in hospital for a few days. My students wanted to know if I had arranged this as a practical demo.

Another time, having just arrived home after teaching the course, I received a phone call from the Commodore of the sailing club. He had just rendered first aid at a RTC on the way home, and it was the first time he had ever come across an accident in all his years of driving, let alone giving first aid; he was so pleased that he had attended that day.

APPENDIX 3

BEING IN CHARGE OF A DIVISION

Running an adult Division like Weybridge, with a number of vehicles and a membership of thirty plus is like trying to run a small business with volunteers. Keeping the money flowing in to pay for the servicing, insurances and then the updating of vehicles, the replacement of medical equipment used on duties as well as uniforms plus the upkeep of the HQ building is quite an art; the turnover of money in any one year is amazing. I would take it personally if someone delayed paying for our services. Once I even complained in writing to London District HQ over non-payment for a large duty (Biggin Hill) and threatened to not attend any more London duties for them. They paid up with the usual "it was an error in the accounts dept".

Eventually I got a nose for knowing the dodgy events, but what really used to annoy me was when I would find out the organisers had paid the Division organising the event who had asked for our help, and then hung onto the monies for six or nine months without passing payment to us. We should have been earning the interest, not them.

As for the members, it's they who make the Division. Some join because their other halves are on shifts and they'd rather not sit at home on their own and some would use us to get first aid training and experience before applying to join the NHS. Iin fact quite a few ended up as paramedics, as well as nurses and even doctors. Others joined because they were looking for friendship, some were just getting over a broken relationship, and we also had a few wannabes -- these people wanted to be instant paramedic or brain surgeon, and usually they did not have the ability to get into the NHS, or could not afford to take the drop in wages. You could spot them a mile off with their all the bits hanging off their belt around their waist and carrying a massive pack on their back. One even asked if he could borrow a defibrillator to go on holiday, just in case he came across a collapse (bless him). The vast majority of the members were loyal and though after a while they may have moved on, I was happy that at least they had a happy experience with us at Weybridge St John.

One thing I learned very early on was that people who moved from Division to Division usually meant trouble, as was the case with the guy from London District I mentioned earlier. Of course if they had moved into our area then this seemed to be OK, but moving from other local Divisions always seemed to end in problems for me.

On one occasion, we had two people transfer and within six months, I found out that they had been meeting down our local pub with two of my existing young members talking about how to get rid of me so they could take over. On the next meeting night at tea break time I announced that I was aware that the meeting had been held and I had news for them -- I was not going, but they were, and promptly marched them into the office. The two new members were asked to hand over their keys and leave. My two members were given a strong talking to. They had the option to remain, which they did; interestingly both later on became paramedics.

I seemed to have problems with anyone called Martin; the first one joined from another Division when Steve Smith was in charge in 1984. He was young and very, very, enthusiastic and thought he knew it all. I turned up one day at the HQ to find the ambulance dashboard in pieces, and there was Martyn with a Y -- that was his nick name -- busy stripping it all apart. I asked him what the hell he was up to as I was the Transport Officer, and he informed me that the vehicle had suffered a complete electrical failure and he was checking it all out. Going back to basics I asked if he had turned off the isolator switch which was what we did when we left it at the HQ. Oooops -- he had not!

Another time Steve rang me to tell me that Martyn had just called him to inform him that he had donated a new set of blankets to the Division. Steve's first comment was "What's he done now?" We soon found out; he had nearly taken out the centre pillar that held up the roof of the garage as he had driven the ambulance out. We did discuss whether we should get rid of him but Steve felt that was admitting defeat, so he stayed though I thought he should go.

It was not until I took over that the opportunity occurred for me to get rid of Martyn. We were at Biggin Hill and he wanted to crew an ambulance and I would not let him as I wanted him on radio control on the unit. He threw a real wobbly and stomped off in a sulk. On returning back to HQ he informed me that he was transferring to a London Division immediately, as he "would be appreciated by them."

By the following evening at Division he told me that he had changed his mind and would be remaining. No he wasn't. I told him I had already sent in his transfer papers that morning and it was too late, (I hadn't but he did not know). Exit one Martyn with a Y.

Although we will always remember the day he was on control and when asked by the LAS to spell a location he pronounced Y as Wankie in stead of Yankee. We could hear them trying to stifle the laughter, then they asked him again to spell it, and again we got Wankie. By this time we were all creased up with laughter and still he could not understand why 'til we explained it to him, then he tried to deny he had said it.

The other Martin was much more of a problem for me. He had met one of my nurses while on duty at Biggin Hill in 1990, and after a while they had become an item. He then transferred to us from London. I did not like this when it happened at Division because from experience I found that if they break up you can often lose one or both of them but he settled in very well and they even got engaged.

The first I knew of trouble was when the Cadet Officer informed me that a mother of a cadet had complained that one of my adult members who was twenty five years old was seeing her fifteen year old daughter. Not only that, but he had written a letter which her mum had found and she was furious and had launched a formal complaint. Guess who it was --- Martin. At first he denied it, but due to the nature of the complaint we convened a board to interview both parties headed by our Commissioner Jill Twamley who was also a JP.

When the letter was produced he had to admit it, though he said she told him she was 17. I had found out that the young lady had been bragging to other members of the cadet Division that she had "pulled" Martin and also had another boyfriend, a 28 year old Firefighter. How do you tell a mother her daughter is not the young innocent girl that she thinks she is -- you can't. In the end Martin was told to resign from Surrey, but when I said that the girl should also resign her mother would not hear of it until I pointed out that no adult would take her out on duty with them in case she accused them of anything. She finally left.

We left Martin to explain to my nurse why he had left as she was unaware of what was going on. After she found out they broke up, and then shortly afterwards she began to be stalked and receive phone calls all times of the day and night by someone but she did not know who. It was much later that she found out it was Martin. In the meantime she'd left us, due to the embarrassment of what had happened, which was a shame as she had enjoyed her time with us.

After sorting out that problem with Cadets, it was a year later that I was again brought into yet another conflict involving the cadets. This time though I had started to receive stories of the Cadet Officer, who had transferred from London, openly smoking in front of the cadets and even encouraging them to smoke with her. Then came the final straw. She took some of the senior cadets to a nightclub in Guildford getting back at two a.m. I spoke to County about the situation and we called a meeting between her and myself and Paul Roots who was then County Staff Officer for Cadets. We were all prepared to have a battle with her but instead she just walked in and said "I'm resigning," and walked out. I felt really deflated after all the work I had put in for the meeting. Her nickname by the way was Spit, though I don't know were it came from.

The final major confrontation occurred in 1999 when a member joined from Oxford. He had moved into the area, had been in St John a few years and also said he was an ex-nurse. He got the nick name of Slug due to his habit of sliding up behind people who were talking and then joining in with the conversation. I met the Commissioner of Oxford while on duty in London and asked her about him, and was told that they were glad to get rid of him as he had caused all sorts of problems, and had moved from Division to Division before moving to Surrey, and to watch him.

He was another one who would not obey orders given by us when on duty. This finally came to a head at a fly-in at Brooklands, when Chris Dunsmore, who was on control, told him to stay on the other side of the flight path with the ambulance until all the aircraft had landed. He decided to ignore the order and return to the unit. Twice Chris told him to stay put but he still came back. Chris was furious and complained to me about the incident. I decided to confront him during the meeting night the next day, and as I was not at the duty, had Chris with me. Also, I was just getting over a heart scare that had happened a month before, so Chris said he would take the lead, and turned up with a clip board with papers on it.

To begin with he tried to justify his action, and then said he did not hear the call, though his crewman confirmed that they had heard it. Then Chris asked him what else we should know about as he looked at the clip board. Well he started to tell us that he had an argument with the police at Princess Diana's funeral, and another argument at this event and that event; there was a lot that was news to us. Then I looked over Chris's shoulder to see what else was on the board, it was BLANK! I then told him that as he had brought the Division and St John into disrepute, I required his keys back and he was out. Though he tried to argue with us he left.

Overall though if you think in sixteen years I only had four major incidents, it was not bad and the majority of the time was spent having a wonderful time with the membership; their loyalty and friendship was second to none. I would never ask them to do anything that I could not do myself.

They say that those who work hard play hard and in Weybridge's case this was so. Getting back to the Old Crown in time after stock-car racing, the Christmas dinners at the beginning of December, the Golden Skull competition held on the last meeting evening of the year, the Blue Lamp award at the AGM for the best cock-up of the year, and New Years parties at the HQ where I even dressed up for one as old father time complete with a beard and a Zimmer frame.

After two years, this event moved to our home at New Haw until the birth of our first child. Now this event has moved to Sam's home; keeping up the tradition. Other events included Sam's surprise 30th birthday party, and Jaynie Signorelli's going away party, (to say good bye as she was off to America to train as a paramedic and then work there). We even organised an American ambulance to collect her from home, the HQ was decorated in red, white and blue -- the white being blown up gloves, and a theme of "This is your Life" with pictures of Jaynie from when she joined at the age of ten.

Also when Sam returned from getting married in St Lucia we threw yet another party, but the members would have to wait until 2002 to get their own back on me. Even Jane was in the know but kept quiet, I turned up to what I thought was a normal meeting night and to my total surprise a "retirement from being the skipper party" had been organised. It was "This is Your Life" night with the "Red Book" and plenty of embarrassment as I mentioned earlier. What a Division!

I had made the decision that after ten years in charge that I would not carry on being there after I was sixty. The Division needed someone younger to run it, and although I tried to train and look for other people to take over it fell to my daughter to do it. She was the obvious choice as she had been in the Division since she was seven years old, but I was not going to just hand it over with out her spending the last year (2001) assisting me on duties, meeting all my contacts and learning the paper work. No way was she going to have what happened to me happen to her, when I inherited a box full of forms and had to learn the hard way.

APPENDIX 4

TRAINING THROUGH INCIDENT EXERCISES

One of the things that had attracted me to Weybridge back in the seventies was their training. A four month programme was always up on the notice board and basics were taught every six weeks with lectures from all sorts of specialist people. A police pathologist one evening showed what they had to do to establish the time of death on a corpse which had lain in a ditch during a hot summer for a few days -- this had involved growing maggots. Another evening, a fire investigation officer showed us what they looked for when investigating suspect arson, and gave some interesting examples of cases. We had talks from the river police, the London Ambulance Service (LAS) and a tour of the LAS control centre at Waterloo.

We attended debriefs of major incidents and as things changed we were kept informed. For example, after the Papa India air crash in 1972, the debrief found that each County ambulance service used a different radio channel including St John, and there were vehicles from London, Surrey, Berkshire as well as us. No one could therefore be in overall control so this led to a change in radio communications. From these debriefs we now today have the inner ring the outer ring at major incidents, Gold,

Silver and Bronze officers, incident, loading and stores officers etc.

The most memorable of all the meetings I went to was in respect of the Moorgate Underground incident that happened in February 1975. Although St John was not involved at all, it was still very interesting to attend. This incident occurred one Friday morning at eight fifty three when a fully loaded commuter train failed to stop at the station and crashed into the dead end of the tunnel killing forty three people. The first thing that came out of this debrief was how no-one knew how many carriages made up a tube train, or how far it was to the end of the tunnel. It was not until the fire-fighters had cleared the first two carriages which were on top of each other that they found the next two were also like it. It would take four and a half days to remove all the bodies. No-one knew that escalators could be reversed, so for the first few hours all the equipment was manually carried down. Likewise, no-one appreciated that the trains move the air around the underground, so when some thing like this happens, heat soon builds up, plus when fire-fighters are using heat cutting equipment to remove the wreckage it soon becomes unbearable. We saw pictures of the dead driver who they reached after two days, but the photo that always sticks in my memory was a city gent sitting on a seat still holding his brief case on his lap but minus his head. He had been decapitated by the window behind him. It was never determined what caused the crash though. The most interesting thing about these sorts of meetings was not how well everyone had done, but what could be learned to improve the management of any further incidents.

Apart from our ongoing training, we also held training exercises, and as I love setting these up and making up the casualties, I was often the main instigator of them. The first one I ever did at Weybridge was in1973; a simulated light air craft crash into the clay hills above the old air raid shelters opposite Vickers at Brooklands. We had invited Windlesham and Bagshot Division to join in as they had the same type of ambulance as us -- a JU 250.

 The only rescue equipment we carried on these vehicles was either a Neil Robertson or a GQ rescue stretcher. We had five casualties in all sorts of inaccessible places on the bank, and we had great evening using the rescue equipment. I always view an exercise as it's the right place to get it wrong -- better in training then in real life, and the more you train with equipment the more confident you are with it.

Not all exercises went to plan though. One held at the Airscrew works the following year, had to be abandoned when then a "worker" who had been crushed by a rolling press and was trapped decided to make it harder for us by moving further into the machine. He then slipped and got totally stuck, and the exercise had to be abandoned while we had to get some engineers to partly dismantle the machine to get him out.

Though you plan for every eventuality, there are times when if it can go wrong it will go wrong. One such event was in the nineties where the scenario involved a capsized sailing dinghy on the Thames and a child (Resus Junior) had been knocked out and was in the water. The boat crew had to find and resus him while on the move on the water and then transfer him to the ambulance on shore.

At the same time two girls had been attacked on the towpath by the river; one had been stabbed and suffered a punctured lung and the other was hysterical. Both were hiding in the undergrowth. The first problem encountered was that the current on the river was a lot faster then I had anticipated and they spent 20 minutes looking for Junior, and finally Mark (acting as a judge on the water) locating him under the branches of a willow tree.

The other first aid team located the girls and after a struggle to treat the stab victim, due to the other girl trying to stop them touching her friend, they loaded her on a stretcher. A member of the public rushed up to say there had just been a stabbing further up the towpath. This was not part of the exercise, it was real! After they dealt with this they returned to find that the towpath was now blocked by an abandoned car.

The following year I set up another exercise by the river and this time a road traffic accident on the nearby river road resulted in us abandoning the exercise again. Then the next year we did an exercise by the river at Weybridge Sailing Club that ended with one of our members while acting drunk, throwing himself through a hedge.

Unfortunately, there was a concrete bollard on the after side and he headbutted it. I received a radio message from one of the teams asking if Patrick was part of the exercise as the make up looked very real. He left St Peters Hospital one hour later with four stitches in a wound .

These incidents were not confined to exercises. A two day RYA power boat course held at Queen Mary's finished early on the assessment afternoon when in a howling gale a club member slipped and fractured their leg while watching the crews being put through their paces slipped, ending up in the water -- our crew now dealt with the real thing.

Sometimes we were invited to take part in exercises organised by Surrey Ambulance or Surrey Fire Service, usually as patients. One of these was held at Fairoaks aerodrome and was a simulated air crash and this would involve being transported to St Peters Hospital for "treatment". I was to be one of the critical casualties and would need to be prioritised and sent with the first batch to hospital. Unfortunately the first on scene were trainee fire-fighters and as the two nearest casualties to me were young girls and making a lot of noise, they decided to treat them first and not assess the whole incident until one of their Officers pointed out their error. I was then carried on a stretcher over burning tyres and dumped at a clearing centre where a medic simulated putting a line in and I was labelled ready for transportation.

As I lay there I heard the noise of a helicopter coming in, and it got louder and louder, I even sat up and watched as a RAF Sea King land near by, then I was loaded onto it. I was still thinking, "Oh well they are just practicing loading" when it took off. What a racket! The vibrations and noise of the engines were deafening but once up in the air and I learned that we were going to fly to St Peters. I was now lying on the floor by the door and I saw the M25 below me when I suddenly thought "Am I insured for this?" Then I heard the pilot say he could not find the hospital (whether this was a wind up or not I don't know) but I then sat up and told one of the crew where it was. We then landed and I was taken to the A&E.

Part of the exercise was to see how the hospital would cope with this sort of incident, and one of the things was that the emergency equipment cupboard was locked and no-one knew who had the key. The casualty triage had fallen apart and they were losing track of casualties. Del boy was acting as a worried relative and causing trouble to such a point that a doctor, who did not appear to be taking the exercise seriously, lost it and told Del go away (or words to that effect) as he did not want people like him there. Del grabbed him and held him against a wall while he explained this could be the actions of a person that is worried about their girlfriend and getting no answers. The best bit of the evening for me though was seeing one of the earlier young girls wandering about in bra and knickers looking for her clothes that had been removed there and then promptly lost.

When they knocked down our HQ, I could not miss the chance of yet another exercise; a gas explosion, working in the rubble looking for casualties. Exercises were held at Queen Mary's sailing club, the rugby club and with us covering Brooklands Museum it was not long before I managed to get their permission to hold exercises there as well -- a simulated heavy landing in a BAC III with one of the members, Elco, a Dutchman acting as the pilot who had banged his head. Halfway through the incident he started to talk in Dutch and it was funny to see our first aiders' reaction.

A heart attack in a Harrier Jump Jet cockpit -- that was fun in trying to get him out, and an air crash on the runway; this was simulated by using two wrecked cars one on top of the other (chained so that they were safe) trays of diesel on fire around the incident and a smoke bomb under the cars. Casualties were supplied by a local amateur dramatic group.

We held another exercise in a underground cellar that was only four feet high and had no lights but lots of spiders. A rolling exercise was fun. This consisted of five incidents and teams would spend fifteen minutes at each. This one came to an abrupt end when some heard a loud "DONG" and shortly afterwards one of the first aiders was found walking in circles; she had walked into the wing of an aeroplane, another one to hospital – concussion.

By far the best exercise I organised though was an Area one. We managed to get permission to use part of Thorpe Park in the closed season. This was a village street and at the time the IRA was active with bombings and this seemed to be a good time to practice a major incident; even the police wanted to take part. The scenario was that two terrorists were at a café on a busy street and one of them was carrying a bomb. This had gone off blowing him apart and injuring twenty five people.

I even had an arm of an Annie hanging from a lamp post still clutching a beer glass (what was left of the bomber). We had eight Divisions taking part. The first ambulance crew made the fatal mistake of starting to treat people and forgot to tell Control of the situation, but with a prompt from us they then let them know and the rest of the vehicles came on site.

My job was to take pictures so I was kept busy until the other bomber walked up to me and asked what he should do as no-one had noticed him.

I knew he had an imitation pistol on him so I suggested that if he wanted, he could start waving it about, which he did. I must say I did not expect and nor did he, the reaction this brought. A police officer struggled with him and a St John member who was treating a casualty rugby tackled him by the legs to the ground, and then the police man held his head to the ground with his boot. I then saw him being handcuffed and thrown into a back of a prison van, at sometime during this he sustained a dislocated shoulder --- oooops! I saw him a few weeks later. He was a baker at a local supermarket and he greeted me with "Don't you ever ask me to be a casualty again." Well I only *suggested* that he waved the gun.

We also attended major incident callouts at Heathrow, but these seemed rather false as we would be parked nearby waiting for the call and the casualties just had labels on them. Once I wrote on one of these labels "treated as per page 32 of the manual".

From the end of 1994, with the introduction of new regulations from National HQ on crewing of our ambulances, we entered a period of training with the emphasis on ambulance work. One of the most memorable trainers was Bill Hinton, an LAS paramedic. His extensive knowledge and ability was only matched by his colourful language, but he was a real basics person and with his and others who taught us by 1995, ten of us qualified as Level 2s and now could legally transport casualties to hospital from our local duties.

In 1997, the members were invited to help out at Ashford Hospital's A & E on Friday nights and the odd Saturday night and a rota was set up with other Divisions. Valuable experience and training was gained by those attending, with them even being allowed to watch minor operations taking place, and in my case one night assisting in replacing a dislocated shoulder. Unfortunately this ended a year later when the Hospital was downgraded and all emergencies then went to St Peters at Chertsey.